D1622385

MORAL EDUCATION
in
Family, School,
and Church

MORAL EDUCATION

in
Family, School,
and Church

by

CHARLES EUGENE CONOVER

THE WESTMINSTER PRESS . *Philadelphia*

LIBRARY OF CONGRESS CATALOG CARD No. 62-10294

PRINTED IN THE UNITED STATES OF AMERICA

TO MY WIFE

CONTENTS

PREFACE

This is a book about morality and moral education. Many significant books have been written in recent years diagnosing the moral crisis of our time, presenting ethical theories—old and new—and interpreting Biblical ethics. Surprisingly little attention, however, has been given to moral education. The writer is convinced that the most neglected aspect of education in America today is moral education. It is not carried on systematically in either the home, the church, or the school. We are not even agreed as to who is responsible for it, let alone what the content of it should be or how it is best carried on.

The term "morality," rather than "ethics," is used in this book because it is not primarily concerned with ethical theory in the philosophical sense, but rather with moral virtue and character, the goals of the moral life, and the principles and standards by which to distinguish right from wrong conduct. The term "education" is used in a broad sense, to include the nurture and training given to children, teaching by example, and counseling of individuals, as well as more formal instruction in morality and ethics.

The intention of the author is to write a book for the persons who carry major responsibilities in moral education— parents, ministers, directors of religious education, teachers, and leaders of youth—rather than for specialists in ethics and theology. The purpose of this book is to study the effectiveness of what we are now doing in moral training and education, to investigate its proper purpose and content, to examine methods and resources available, and to ask what contributions should be expected from institutions such as the family, the school, and the church. It is the writer's objective to bring knowledge and insights from various disciplines to bear upon these problems rather than to present a new ethical theory or educational philosophy. His responsibilities as a teacher and counselor have led him to give his major attention to the interpretation of morality and religion for college students. A growing awareness that the decisive influences upon values and character are usually exerted before the college years, and that more emphasis should be placed upon preparing parents and teachers for the moral training of children, is among the reasons for this survey of the problems of moral education from the earliest to the adult years of life.

Four chapters of this book first took form as lectures prepared for adult groups in the St. Charles and Normandy, Missouri, Presbyterian churches, and for a course in Christian ethics taught at Lindenwood College by the writer and by Assistant Professor Mary Jean Bartholomew. Lively and helpful discussions that followed the lectures encouraged the writing of these chapters for publication. William West Thomas, a colleague in the Department of Philosophy and Religion at Lindenwood College, read the manuscript and made valuable suggestions concerning language and style. My wife, the first reader of these chapters, helped greatly with the content and style of this book.

C. E. C.

CHAPTER I

MORALS AND MORAL EDUCATION IN AMERICA TODAY

1. MORAL RESPONSIBILITIES OF THE PRESENT AND THE FUTURE

There are compelling reasons today for turning our attention to morality and moral education. The future of mankind is at stake; that future depends primarily upon the character, the convictions, and the goals of the peoples of the world. Even the best and wisest of us are perplexed by responsibilities that are now inescapable. These include avoidance of suicidal nuclear war, the continuation of the struggle against Communist domination of the world, and the extension of areas of agreement and co-operation among the nations of the world. Prof. F. S. C. Northrop, of Yale University, has pointed to the disturbing fact that the most civilized nations are the most dangerous to civilization:

> Ours is a paradoxical world. The achievements which are its glory threaten to destroy it. The nations with the highest standard of living, the greatest capacity to take care of their people economically, the broadest education, and the most enlightened morality and religion, exhibit the least capacity to avoid mutual destruction in war. It would seem that the more civilized we become, the more incapable of maintaining civilization we are.[1]

The moral responsibilities of the present call for new kinds and new levels of training and education, and for forms of morality and religion that protect rather than endanger the human race.

The future will bring even greater responsibilities, if we avoid the immediate dangers before us. New moral obligations are appearing with the extension of human activities into space, the growth of the world's population toward an estimated six billions of persons in the year 2000 and seventy billions by the twenty-fifth century, and increasing scientific powers over men's bodies and minds.

Even if there were no indications of moral crisis within American life today, we would be under obligation to give the most thoughtful and creative consideration to the changes in moral education needed to prepare young people as wisely as possible for the responsibilities they will assume and the unforeseeable decisions they will make. But we have in addition a wide range of evidence that our present training and instruction in morality and ethics prepares our youth inadequately even for the ordinary personal and social responsibilities and obligations of civilized existence.

Some of the evidences of moral failure, especially in the inner areas of our metropolitan centers, seem alarming indeed: crimes of violence, increases in drug addiction and alcoholism, illegitimate births, marriage failures, persistence of prejudice against and segregation of minority groups, extreme disciplinary problems in some of our schools, and difficulties in maintaining honest political processes and effective government. What is implied for moral training by the present situation, in which more children are growing up in the slums of our cities than on our farms, is yet to be determined. Social agencies, various branches of governments, churches, and schools are dealing realistically with the problems of areas of our civilization where children and adults are economically, culturally, and emotionally underprivileged; thus far they have had quite limited success.

Other indications of our need for more effective moral education are found on our college and university campuses, where there are scandals in athletics and reports of widespread dishonesty in examinations. This is also true of high schools in privileged communities, and there are indications that delinquent and criminal behavior is spreading to areas that were once largely immune to such influences. Examples of unethical practices on the part of business and professional leaders and government officials are frequently reported in the press. A recent survey of businessmen indicates that four out of five executives admit that one or more unethical practices are "common" in their fields of business.[2]

Fortunately, there are also many encouraging aspects of American life. Juvenile delinquents are a minority of our young people, and many of our citizens are devoting themselves to the correction of injustices and to the public welfare. Historian Henry Steele Commager calls our attention to the growth of humanitarianism in treatment of prisoners, in working conditions, in concern for minority groups, and to the increase of tolerance in religion, politics, and daily life.[3] We establish agencies and foundations for all sorts of commendable purposes. We continue to be concerned about the freedom, dignity, and opportunities of the individual. With the assistance of the Russians, we are increasingly serious about education and scientific research. An increasing proportion of our aid to other countries is planned to help them achieve higher standards of living. Our scientists display a keen social conscience. Government officials are wrestling with ethical problems in their own work, and establishing regulations to protect consumers from unethical practices in business. Business and professional groups are preparing codes of ethics to guide their own conduct. The moral situation calls for concern, for thoughtful analysis and constructive response, rather than for pessimism.

The most useful clues to what we are now doing and failing to do in moral education are to be found among the searching studies of the attitudes and beliefs of college students made recently with particular reference to the influence of institutions of higher learning upon student values and character. These young people have been most responsive to our program of education, and they include a large proportion of the members of their generation who will significantly influence the cultural forms of the future. The writer's experience as a teacher and counselor on college and university campuses convinces him that students quite accurately reflect and represent the culture of our time; his own students have accepted as basically correct the analysis of the campus situation that is given in the next section.

2. THE CAMPUS MORAL SITUATION

There are many reasons for pride and confidence in the students now in our colleges and universities. They are frank in expressing their opinions and realistic in their approach to the world; the majority of them are serious about succeeding in their educational careers and finding useful and secure places in the world. They are, as Philip E. Jacob reports in *Changing Values in College*, "dutifully responsive to government," though not enthusiastic about political processes and responsibilities.[4] There are volunteers for the Peace Corps and for dangerous assignments in exploration in space and other scientific undertakings. On our campuses there is a concern for human rights and a sense of need for religion. There is no dearth of serious and able campus leaders.

Yet it is also true that the moral climate is changing, and administrators in colleges and universities face increasing disciplinary problems. In part this may be an inevitable result of extending the privileges of higher education to wider segments of the population. In part it seems to be an indication of change in our values and in the role of morality and religion in our lives, with important implications for moral education.

One characteristic of the campus moral situation is the belief, especially prevalent among students as they first come to the college campus, that morality is a personal and private matter. It is not that moral standards are entirely repudiated but that they are considered as relative to individual preferences. A student may say: "What he is doing is contrary to my principles. However, I will not criticize him, for he thinks that it is right." The imperative character of the basic moral principles, and their essentially social nature, is not apparent to large numbers of our students. One of the results is difficulty in establishing and maintaining honor systems in the areas of examinations and campus social regulations. Such systems require both universal acceptance of the obligations involved and impartial enforcement of honor codes.

For some years, in a course in ethics, the writer has asked students to comment on the case of Betty, a major in education who copied reports prepared by another student and presented them as her own. When her dishonesty was discovered, she defended her action, without explaining her motives, before a disciplinary board. "I copied these reports, and it was right that I do so in my situation. Since I think that my action is right, I should not be punished." But not many students see the seriousness of the moral issues involved for society when a prospective teacher publicly defends dishonesty, and for the institution if such conduct is considered permissible because professedly conscientious. This is a representative student comment: "I believe that Betty should be admired rather than punished for admitting the truth and also for standing up for what she believed was right. Because she believed she had done the right thing, she shouldn't be punished." The findings of Philip E. Jacob are similar:

> The traditional moral virtues are valued by almost all students. But they are not inclined to censor those who choose to depart from these canons. Nor do they feel personally bound to unbending consistency in observing the code, especially when a lapse is socially sanctioned.[5]

Conformity to what is expected by others, especially within the peer group, is a second characteristic of students, especially in the high school and earlier college years. The Purdue University Opinion Polls, reporting answers from 8,000 to 15,000 high school students in grades nine to twelve, give evidence of the importance of group membership in the adolescent years.

Twenty-six per cent say: "More than anything I want to be accepted as a member of the group that is most popular at school." . . . Fifty per cent feel greatly upset if the group doesn't approve of them. . . . Fifty-one per cent try very hard to do everything that will please their friends.[6]

Studies of the influence of institutions of higher education on the values and the character of students show that the campus student life and culture limits the influence of the faculty and the curriculum. John Bushnell, in his extensive interviews with Vassar students, found the campus peer group to be the basis of campus status and security, the chief authority concerning what to believe and how to act, and a powerful influence in showing new students how to keep the faculty at a distance and to discourage "genuine relationships of a kind that might challenge the basic values of the students."[7] The student culture is more representative of American culture in general than of the culture represented by faculty members. The increasing authority of this "adolescent subculture," as Dean Thomas S. Hall, of Washington University,[8] has named it, is a clue to the diminishing influence of the family during the school and college years as well as of our schools and colleges, and has a significant bearing upon the problems of moral education for the future.

The campus moral situation has a paradoxical character. Morality is viewed as a matter that each person should decide for himself, yet at the same time there is a marked tendency to conform to what others are doing — especially when moral standards are being relaxed. "If everyone else cheats," said a student, "why shouldn't I?" It should be noted that this taking of one's moral bearings with reference to what others are doing is not limited to students. "I'm just doing what everybody is doing" is a statement frequently heard among adults, including active church members.

Relativistic individualism and group conformity are not

contradictory. They have a common basis: a lack of moral standards which the individual is obliged to defend and obey and by which the group is to be judged. In such a situation, traditional moral principles have lost their binding character. William Lee Miller has correctly diagnosed the problem and has indicated where the solution lies:

> Much of the contemporary criticism of "conformity" . . . seems off the point, for it implicitly or explicitly recommends "individualism" or "autonomy" against the "crowd," when actually a relativistic individualism, exalting each man's opinion and desire, is the chief source of the "conformity." Essentially, the problem is not created by the individual's refusing to oppose the crowd; it is found in the individual's taking so little interest in discovering what is right. It is not that we Americans may have lost a sense of individuality; it is rather that we may lose a sense of the mind's connection with reality.[9]

A third characteristic of students is that the majority of them are self-oriented. Charles Morris, after studying the world's religions, devised a questionnaire that has been used in various countries. Each student was asked to state his own philosophy of life through indicating the degree of his liking or disliking of thirteen different "ways of living." A significant pattern appears in the average ratings of American students. Highest place is given to a flexible approach to life's good things: "integrate action, enjoyment, and contemplation." Their conservatism appears in the second choice: "preserve the best that man has achieved." American activism characterizes the next two ways approved: "constantly master changing conditions," and "chance adventuresome deeds." Even their participation in groups is egocentric, for "enjoy life through group participation" is ranked higher than "show sympathetic concern for others."[10] This value pattern is that of the person who is more interested in what society offers him than in what he can contribute to others. John Bushnell found that while

Vassar students expect to fulfill their womanhood as wives and mothers, "the vast majority of our subjects have no ambitions whatever in terms of making an enduring contribution to our society."[11]

It is not surprising that students think primarily of themselves. Shepard B. Clough, in *Basic Values of Western Civilization,* maintains that our culture places the development of the individual at the very base of our value system and glorifies the individual.[12] Educational institutions, too, focus upon the individual, assisting him to achieve self-understanding and to prepare for his career. And the majority of students have not yet experienced the loyalties and responsibilities that are most likely to rescue us from egocentricity in marriage and the family, in work and community activities. Yet this egotistical approach is a significant clue to the place of morality and religion in our lives today, and it is a matter of concern when the great issues are social and the future of the world hangs in the balance.

A fourth element in the campus moral situation is that morality is experienced and interpreted in its negative character of restraint far more than in its positive significance as the way to the fullest development of persons and of society. This is due in part to the prominence of prohibitions in our moral training and in campus regulations. We cannot rely upon regulations and laws to provide positive motivations and purposes. Bernard Mayo suggested that the function of laws "is not to get people to *do* what they would not do if left to themselves, but to stop them from doing what they *would* do if left to themselves."[13] Student attitudes toward moral principles and campus rules indicate a dominantly hedonistic approach in the areas of relations between the sexes and the use of alcohol. Both in matters of personal conduct and of the basic requirements of a society, the contributions of morality to the greater good of human beings have not been made clear. One of the evidences of this is that many students are more concerned with escaping detection and punishment than they are with personal character, reputation, or social consequences. "I'll take my chances," they say.[14]

A fifth characteristic of student behavior is that other values tend to take precedence over moral considerations. Our problem is not that traditional moral standards are openly rejected but rather that individual purposes and the behavior patterns in the group to which the student is adjusting frequently outweigh the moral norms. Problems concerning honor and honesty are particularly revealing illustrations of the moral situation. Dishonesty in examinations and plagiarism mean rejection of the process of learning which is the purpose of the process of education, repudiation of the integrity essential to the scholar, and introduction of injustice and unreliability into the procedures for selecting and recommending young people for responsible positions in society. The extent of dishonesty is disturbing. Confidential reports from college and university students show that from 11 to 49 per cent of the students admit having cheated at least once. The authors of *What College Students Think* found that 37 per cent of the students polled admit having cheated, and they believe that their findings understate the problem.[15] A survey made in a large and respected high school indicates that 90 per cent of the students are involved in cheating on homework, quizzes, tests, or examinations.[16] A student's explanation of campus dishonesty is perceptive: "We're success-oriented; so we figure that it's all right to cheat in order to succeed; that's the problem."[17] The subsidiary role of moral values could not be more clearly stated.

A sixth characteristic of college students is their satisfaction with America as it is now, or as it can be with such modifications as racial equality. To the question asked by John Bushnell, "What is your conception of the ideal society?" Vassar students in general answered that utopia is impossible, and that our society is about as ideal as any could be.[18] Where changes were suggested, they were largely expressions of personal need for more freedom, or encouragement, or support.

Optimistically, they think that the wrongs in our society will gradually right themselves. This satisfaction with American life is substantiated in other studies of the campus; according to the authors of *What College Students Think,* it does not mean that students are unaware of the conflicts and dangers of the world today. A student said, "I guess one of the things that bothers us is that there is no great issue that we feel we can personally come to grips with." They discover little that they can do about the world situation, and they find that they must criticize some of the results of the liberal movements of the recent American past. They see no desirable alternatives to this present situation:

> If, then, they are conservatives and apathetic, they are so, in part, by default. There are no clearly defined programs around which to rally, no clearly defined answers to the problems their generation confronts. In social psychological terms we would say that they react to baffling complexity by withdrawing. In the slogan of their own campus culture they "play it cool."[19]

The attitudes of college students also provide important clues to our religious situation today. The great majority of students believe in God, and say that they need a religious orientation to provide meaning for their lives. But religion as well as morality tends to be a personal and private matter. And, significantly, religion does not seem to make a difference in the moral life. Philip E. Jacob has described the secular character of campus life, despite student interest in religion and church attendance:

> There is a "ghostly quality" about the beliefs and practices of many of them. . . . Their religion does not carry over to guide and govern important decisions in the secular world. Students expect these to be socially determined. God has little to do with the behavior of men in society, if widespread student judgment be accepted. His place is in church and perhaps in the home, not in business or club

or community. He is worshiped, dutifully and with propriety, but the campus is not permeated with a live sense of his presence.[20]

Religion, as well as morality, is changing. It is not only that these two aspects of our life, almost inseparably connected for so long, are increasingly divorced from each other and from the considerations that influence the most important decisions. It is also true, if the campus is indicative of the direction of change, that religion is increasingly humanistic, rather than theistic or cosmic. The only "way of living" in the Morris list which includes a cosmic reference and calls for obedience was decisively rejected by American students.[21] More direct and recent evidence of a humanistic trend is found in *What College Students Think*. While 75 per cent of the students interviewed in eleven universities believe in God, what they report as their religious experience is a "sense of belongingness," a feeling of collective identity rather than an experience of the reality of a transcendent Being. They feel that their own church "has its own personality, something over and above the individual members in it." Some associate this mystical character with a local congregation, some with their form of religion.[22] While the majority of Roman Catholic students seek traditional religious values, Jewish and Protestant students at Cornell University place "personal adjustment," "family," "intellectual clarity," and "community feeling" ahead of God, prayer, salvation, and the church as "the requirements of an ideal religious or ethical system." As the authors of this book point out, these "are secular values rather than sacred ones."[23]

It is in the light of such evidences of a changing moral and religious situation on our campuses that these words of Philip E. Jacob carry their full impact:

> Perhaps these students are forerunners of a major cultural and ethical revolution, the unconscious ushers of an essentially secular (though nominally religious), self-oriented (though group-conforming) society.[24]

If morality is seen as a personal matter, and decisions are made with reference to individual advantage or group standards, and if religion brings belongingness and personal adjustment rather than an experience of the holy and "a divine imperative," then we are in the midst of a revolutionary change in our values in which the obligations traditionally recognized as binding upon us no longer hold.

The values of students on various college and university campuses across the United States, investigators report, are remarkably similar. This fact points to the culture as the chief influence upon students' goals and standards. Charles Morris investigated determining factors in value preferences. He found that psychological factors such as temperament and character, and biological factors such as age, sex, and body size, are not alone sufficient to account for the persistence of certain patterns in the choices expressed in the ratings of "ways of living." Furthermore, variations in religious backgrounds of the parents make little difference in the preferences shown by students, and differences are no greater between the students from families with religious affiliations and those without. Professor Morris stated his conclusion in *Varieties of Human Value:*

> Perhaps the most striking fact about the means of the ratings of the thirteen ways is the degree of their stability over the various regions of a culture. The rank order of the means in various parts of the United States is much the same, and the same is generally also true for China and India. This suggests that the main determinant of the ratings is a social one, that modes of life deemed desirable by individuals are the modes of life approved in the culture to which they belong.[25]

The moral and religious situation on our college and university campuses indicates a changing value pattern in America. Traditional moral and religious beliefs and principles are not repudiated. But they are not central and authoritative.

The major influence in this change seems to be American culture. A brief examination of the changing pattern of values in our common life is needed to complete our account of the background and problems of moral education today.

3. Changing Value Patterns in American Culture

If American culture is the major influence in the moral and religious revolution becoming clearly evident in our time, an examination of our values should provide the context for a realistic consideration of the content and methods of moral education for the future. The term "values" is used here in a descriptive rather than in a normative sense. What do Americans really care about, prefer, strive for, expect satisfaction from, today? What do we want to become, as individuals, and as a society? And what changes in our valuations are discernible?

The "realm" of values is wide and rich, difficult to outline and describe, and impossible to divide into neat categories that are mutually exclusive. But values do tend to appear in clusters rather than singly, and in recognizable areas of human life such as the realms of economics, politics, and religion. Shepard B. Clough points out that each culture has its distinctive way of life.

> The total galaxy of ways of doing things and looking at things, weighted according to their respective standing in a culture, constitute the value pattern of the culture.[26]

There are "foundation" realms of value essential to the continuation of life and to the support of "higher" values, such as we find in the arts and sciences. One of these fundamental value clusters has its focus in the biological aspects of man's nature and existence. It includes life, pleasure and pain in their physiological basis and dimensions, sex, reproduction, health, and the prevention and cure of disease, infirmities, and suffering. Strong drives, needs, and desires are found here: hunger, sex impulses, love of life, the search for pleasure and the avoidance of pain, the quest for health and strength, the physical requirements of nurture of the young, the needs for human assistance and companionship. The bases of institutions — the family, the community, the economy, the political order—are found here. These values appear in every age, though emphases change. Henri Bergson pointed to one characteristic emphasis of our time when he wrote that "sex appeal is the keynote of our whole civilization."[27] Moral problems in this realm of physical values are increasingly difficult to solve. Science is making possible a rapid increase in the world's population through control of the causes of death, and, at the same time, presenting new dangers to human germ plasm and health from radiation, and to human existence from nuclear war.

Economic values form a second basic cluster. At least a minimum of economic goods is necessary for life, health, human dignity, freedom, and leisure for the enjoyment of the full range of human satisfaction and achievement. Changes are clearly apparent in the economic realm. The Puritan values of work, of pride of craftsmanship, of thrift, of individual achievement, and of serving God in and through daily life reflect a situation in which economic goods were scarce and production was largely an individual or family matter. Mass production; mass consumption; "bigness" and concentration of power in great corporations and labor unions; automation and technical efficiency; social security; credit cards; "planned obsolescence"; "featherbedding"; "expense accounts"; a growing economy; an ever-higher standard of living; highly organized research; the pressure of sales techniques; concern for the stock market; the business index; the level of unemployment; and governmental controls of many kinds in the economic area— all are marks of an economic system clearly different from that in which classical economic theory, with its emphasis upon the private entrepreneur and an unregulated market, took form. Identical bids from competing manufacturers seem to indicate a movement away from competition but toward a "live and let live" economic morality. The requirements of a highly organized economy leave little place for "rugged individualists." It is not surprising that economic values receive so much of our attention and elicit so much of our effort. The American economy is so successful in producing an immense variety of products, in giving tangible indications of "progress," in stimulating desires to possess its products, that it has a major share of our attention. The welfare of the family and our other institutions is bound up with the gross national product and the rate of employment. Money is the key not only to economic goods but also to cultural goods. And money is, to a significant degree, the measure of success and status in American society, and the way to acceptance and status. Our "materialism" is not a simple phenomenon. It is, as Reinhold Niebuhr has pointed out, in part a delight in technical efficiency and in keeping our production facilities busy. It is, as Santayana recognizes, not love of money for its own sake:

> The American talks about money, because that is the symbol and measure he has at hand for success, intelligence, and power; but as to the money itself he makes, spends, loses, and gives it away with a very light heart. To my mind the most striking expression of his materialism is his singular preoccupation with quantity.[28]

It is, nevertheless, the case that the values associated with the economic order tend to outweigh other values, including moral standards. Truth, justice, integrity of the product, fair practices in employment and in strikes, tend to give way to what is expedient and successful. The market orientation tends to spread into the professions, into educational institutions, into sports, and even into religious institutions, which must also make progress and "succeed" in measurable terms. Crime is often a short cut to economic goods, taken at the expense of legal and moral considerations. Max Lerner points to the danger in our preoccupation with this realm of values and its associated types of status and satisfaction.

In America the cultural life goods—success, competition, power, prestige, security, happiness—speak more loudly than the moral codes. The indices of belonging are belongings. What gives a person status is less integrity than success; what drives him is the emulation of the possessors; what is likely to fill his thoughts is not the right way of life but new access to the goods of life.[29]

As our economy reaches new levels of efficiency and productive capacity, the emphasis seems to be shifting from the citizen as worker and producer to the citizen as customer and consumer. This is not an economy dedicated to "economy" in the traditional sense of thrift and conservation of resources. It encourages us to "enjoy now and pay later," to yield to our desires to possess instead of developing what in moral terms is called self-control or temperance, but in economic terms is called "sales resistance." The privileges and satisfactions of the consumer tend to outweigh the responsibility and discipline of the worker. In the words of the Rockefeller Panel:

> The characteristic picture of the citizen as consumer has taken a firm grip on the national imagination; and the consumer is, almost by definition, a creature devoted to self-gratification. He must be constantly and ingeniously served milder cigarettes, softer mattresses, and easier-driving cars. If his dollars are to continue flowing, he must be endlessly catered to, soothed, anointed, protected, healed, cajoled, and generally babied.[30]

The "privatism" of college students, as their self-interest has been called, widens this consumer attitude into a general approach to life. Our moral and religious tradition, the pressing demands of the world situation for national integrity and strength, and the urgent needs of a vastly increased world population in the future, call for reassessment of our economy and of its goal of producing increasing quantities of things for private consumption. And an examination of the distribution of rewards and honors in our society is in order. An encouraging number—48 per cent—of men in universities indicated a strong desire to find work that will permit them to be creative and original, but they expect smaller rewards in terms of income and recognition than if they had chosen less-demanding fields.

Indications of change are also evident in our next cluster of values, which centers in romance, marriage, and the family. "Dating" and marriage occur at an earlier age than they did in previous generations, and we have high expectations of happiness and security in marriage and in family life. Despite the failure of one third of our marriages, we continue to stress romantic love much more than we do moral considerations, such as character, fidelity, and maturity, as the basis of happy marriages. Nevertheless, many American families are held together by strong ties of affection and shared interests, of responsibility and readiness to make sacrifices for other members, as well as by dependence upon shared economic resources.

Many of the functions formerly exercised by the family are being transferred to other institutions. No longer the productive unit in our economy, save in exceptional cases, relying upon school and college, church and "character-building agencies" for the basic educational tasks from nursery school through the graduate school, the family is dependent upon other institutions. Increasing participation of married women in work outside the home and our highly organized community life pull the members of the family into separate, rather than joint, activities.

From the standpoint of its influence upon our values, the family remains an institution of central importance. The cultural level of the families in which they are nurtured largely determines what levels of the rich values of our culture children come to appreciate. Any thorough study of American life must deal with the very different levels of culture and status, from the least to the most privileged, which are found among us, with their differences in morality, religion, interest in education, cultural values, and responsible participation in community life. Different families make different aspects of our complex culture accessible; as Fairchild and Wynn express it in *Families in the Church,* "cultural values are screened through family filters and do not come to the young child directly."[31] The family therefore continues to play a very important mediating role in the induction of children into their cultural heritage and environment.

But the influence of the family is declining, at least in the moral and religious realms. The world penetrates the life of the home through the almost continuous influence of television and other mass means of communication, and through the pressure of the peer culture in the adolescent years. The family is expected to supply cars and other "status symbols" for young people. Margaret Mead points to the revolutionary implications of the present situation in which the family takes its moral bearings from what is being done, and what is expected, in the community around it.

> When mothers cease to say, "When I was a girl I was not allowed . . ." and substitute the question, "What are the other girls doing?" something very fundamental has happened to the whole culture.[32]

This change involves a shift in moral authority from the parents as interpreters of the moral tradition to the groups to which members of the family wish to belong.

The next cluster of values is found in the area of our political institutions, ideals, and loyalties. Limitations upon the powers of government for the sake of life, liberty, and the pursuit of happiness for the individual citizen are traditionally expected and defended by Americans. A suspicion of government persists. Our motto, someone said, is "In God we trust, in government we mistrust." Yet the powers and functions of government, especially upon the national level, are increasing. There is evidence that our political philosophy as well as our practice is changing. We can best understand these changes, and their implications for morality and religion, by examining first the nineteenth-century form of American political beliefs and attitudes.

Three doctrines form the central core of the American democratic faith, according to Ralph Henry Gabriel, who has written a comprehensive account of *The Course of American Democratic Thought:*

> Nineteenth-century Americans affirmed, as the primary doctrine of their democratic faith, that beneath society, its customs and institutions, a law exists that men did not make. This law outlines the patterns of both individual and social life. For the individual it establishes the principles on which to found a beneficent and constructive life. For society it institutes an order within which persons may grow in understanding and in virtue.[33]

Constitutionalism in government is an expression of the primacy of law; the doctrine of the moral law assumes that principles of universal validity underlie the rights of free men and the laws which govern their conduct. Abraham Lincoln is representative of the type of democratic leader who can be trusted with responsibility and wartime powers because he obeys the fundamental moral law.

The second doctrine of the democratic faith is that of the dignity, freedom, and power of the individual citizen.

> Power, of necessity, implied responsibility; responsibility suggested something above the individual to which he must be responsible. The aphorism, liberty under law, stated in political terms the doctrine of the free individual.[34]

Our traditional doctrine is not that the individual is free to do as he pleases; it holds that the more men understand and follow the moral law, the less they need control by man-made laws and government. The doctrine of progress was also stated in moral terms.

This philosophy affirmed that the advance of civilization

is measured by the progress of men in apprehending and translating into individual and social action the eternal principles of right and justice.[35]

The third doctrine of the democratic faith is the "mission of America to cherish and to hold steadfastly before the nations the ideal of the free and self-governing individual."[36] This belief reflects not only the optimism of the Age of Reason, but also in secular form the millennial hopes of evangelical religious groups. The democratic faith, as Gabriel clearly sees, "was a formulation of a religion of nationalism."[37] In the nineteenth century it was not a rival of the dominantly Christian worship of God; rather, these secular and religious faiths complemented each other.

> Together they provided the American with a theory of the cosmos which gave significance and direction to human life, and with a theory of society which gave a meaning not only to the relation of the individual to the group, but of the United States to the congregation of nations.[38]

These three doctrines of the American democratic faith persist in changing form amidst a changing nation and world. The individual continues to be valued. Shepard B. Clough holds that the West is unique in "placing the development of the individual at the very base of our value system," and in "glorifying" individual man. Not only the welfare state but education and even religion serve man:

> The basic purpose of man in the West is neither to honor a deity or deities, nor to sacrifice the individual to the advancement of some social institution such as the national state. Ours is a humanistic view. The masterpiece of man is "better man," living in a "better society," partaking of a "fuller" life, and producing and enjoying more of what we consider to be the "finer" things of life.[39]

But despite our individualism, the functions and powers of the government have greatly increased, extending into the educational and economic areas as the requirements of military strength and security increase. Professor Clough sees that the nation-state, which bears much of the blame for our world wars, threatens much of our value system, but he is optimistic concerning our abilities to change our institutions.[40]

The possibility of an idolatrous American nationalism exists today, for intense nationalistic feelings were generated in World War I and stimulated in the struggles with fascist and communist movements. When existing alongside vital forms of universal religion worshiping a transcendent God, and when morality effectively checks excesses both of individuals and society, the American democratic faith provides national unity and purpose within moral and constitutional limits, and a concern for the freedom and welfare of other nations. If, however, studies of our college students and of our cultural value structure are correct in reporting a revolution toward humanism in religion and toward conformity to society in morality, the resources for the modification of nationalism are decreasing and the dangers of an American form of totalitarianism increasing.

The next cluster of values centers around education, the intellectual life, science, and the fine arts. The importance of education to the individual and to the nation is evident, and increasing sums of money are spent on our schools and on institutions of higher learning. Professor Clough notes that colleges and universities are the real "temples" of Western culture, and that in recent times educational buildings rank immediately after business buildings in impressiveness and importance.[41] The level of education an individual reaches determines to a large extent the range and "height" of the cultural values open to him. While higher education is often sought for its instrumental values in terms of preparation for desirable business and professional positions, it makes our human heritage available, opening the way to understanding of science and philosophy and theology and appreciation of the fine arts.

One of the most disturbing aspects of our present situation is the limited influence of the men and women who are on the frontiers of human knowledge, creativity, and insight: the scientists, the artists, the philosophers, and the theologians. It is not only that vast numbers of our people, including many college graduates, are influenced chiefly by popular and superficial forms of culture; it is also that even the university is so departmentalized that each specialized group speaks largely to its own members. Robert Oppenheimer tellingly expresses this predicament from the scientist's point of view:

> To put it with great brutality, the point is that the scientist is not in society today, any more than is the artist or the philosopher.

> Of course, he does get paid, he does get patronized and even for odd reasons that he sometimes does not understand, rejected. But he is not in society, in the sense that the ideas he has, the work he is doing, stop really rather short with the limits of his profession. They are not part of the intellectual and cultural life of the times. I am over and over again appalled by how ignorant, how incredibly ignorant of the most rudimentary things about my subject are my fellows the historians, my acquaintances the statesmen, my friends the men of affairs. They have no notion of what cooks in physics; I think they have very little notion of what cooks in any other science. And I know that only by good luck and some hard work do I have even a rudimentary notion of what cooks in other parts of the house called science than the one I live in.[42]

Each specialized field faces this difficulty in speaking to and influencing our culture. And each branch of knowledge is more complex, more difficult to understand, more divided than in previous generations. The direct and immediate influences upon our values are more likely to come from the value clusters previously considered than from the arts and sciences.

It would, however, be misleading to conclude that the influence of science upon our values and our future is indirect only. Applied science brings such changes in our human powers and ways of living that it presents us with new and increasingly difficult moral and political problems as well as with new possibilities for unprecedented human welfare. Not only is it increasing our mastery over nature, for either creative or destructive endeavors; it is also providing us with knowledge and techniques for controlling and modifying man himself. Terms such as "engineering of consent" and "brainwashing" suggest the moral and political dangers before us. And at the same time the high evaluation we place on the clarity and verifiability of scientific hypotheses, and on continual progress in knowledge and power over nature by the scientific method, presents difficulties in the areas of morality and religion. When, as in logical empiricism in philosophy, verification in sense experience becomes the criterion of meaningfulness, and the scientific method becomes the only rational approach to reality, then metaphysics and poetry, moral judgments and belief in God, are viewed as factually meaningless and basically irrational. In such a philosophy, science becomes the center of a naturalistic and humanistic reorganization of our beliefs and attitudes, faiths and hopes. Ethical theories and theologies, moral and religious education, must come to terms with science, which is the major factor in changes in knowledge, ways of living, and ways of thinking about the universe. The principal issue is between those who believe that morality and religion must be reconstructed, with man as the center and scientific method as the only reliable criterion, and those who continue to find their ultimate standard and loyalty in response to what they believe to be God's self-revelation.

When we examine the moral cluster of values, it is not surprising that college students and others are confused about the nature and function of morality. Our heritage is mixed and inconsistent. It includes the Greek values of courage, temperance, wisdom, and justice, the Stoic emphasis upon self-control, the Epicurean search for peace of mind, and the common man's search for exciting pleasures. The Christian emphasis upon love for God and man is in tension with the individual and competitive approach of laissez-faire economics, and with the present demand for conforming "organization men." A remarkable variety of moral, immoral, and nonmoral models is presented to youth, ranging from the heroes and villains of our Western frontier to movie stars, astronauts, millionaires, athletes, entertainers, gangsters, industrialists, military leaders, scientists, and statesmen. A thoughtful young person may well come to the conclusion that we have not made up our minds as to what kind or kinds of persons we admire and value most. As Charles Morris has said, we are now engaged in a struggle to define the type of man who is to be given preferred status in our society.[43] The moral situation is, in truth, revolutionary.

The expectations of our society also give grounds for confusion concerning our moral obligations. Honor, honesty, responsibility, and self-control are among the traditional ideals we teach. But another list of characteristics, more indicative of adjustment to the group than of morality, is rated very high today. John Bushnell's interviews with students reveal an emphasis now not so much upon moral virtues as on agreeableness, friendliness, co-operativeness, acceptance of others, general ease of relationship. The interviewers whose work is reported in *Americans View Their Mental Health* asked people to identify qualities in themselves of which they are proud, and in which they consider themselves to be different from other people; their findings are similar:

> The strong points most people mention fall into the category of the stereotyped virtues; they regard themselves as good churchgoers, providers, housewives. In other words, they judge themselves in the light of their ability to come to terms with the external world rather than their ability to deal with their inner conflicts and personal problems.

This suggests that most of us are preoccupied with conforming to accepted standards of behavior and that it is difficult for us to construct our own individual values and be guided by them when they differ from the expectations of our fellows.[44]

The final, traditionally "highest" cluster consists of religious values. A rapid growth of membership in our churches has occurred in recent years without the evidences of moral renewal which in earlier centuries accompanied such religious movements as that in England and America under the leadership of John Wesley. It is not on college and university campuses alone that we find piety combined with dominantly secular attitudes. Recently a Jewish scholar wrote on *Religious Revival and Moral Crisis*,[45] and a Protestant denomination adopted a report entitled *Church Membership Up, Moral Standards Down*.[46] When faith no longer has an evident influence on moral character and conduct, we must conclude that there have been marked changes in our religious values.

Moral education and movements for moral reform in our time must take place within a complex and shifting pattern of values and of life. The changes in our lives, and the accompanying new moral problems such as euthanasia, come largely from new scientific knowledge which is applied in other realms, such as the economy and medicine. Economic and governmental institutions are increasing in complexity and influence, and we are increasingly dependent upon them. The family and educational institutions reflect this dependence, though the functions and influence of the family are decreasing while those of educational institutions are growing. But despite the expansion of educational institutions, our cultural leaders have far less influence on the majority of our citizens than does the commercially controlled popular content of our mass means of communication. The moral standards by which both individual conduct and institutional policies have been judged, and the religious institutions which proclaim an obligation higher than that to the nation-state, are declining in authority and influence, though they are not rejected.

The value patterns of college students are consonant with those of our culture. When the moral climate is confusing and we are uncertain of the content, methods, and goal of moral education, it is to be expected that students will see morality as a private and personal matter. When the family, educational institutions, and churches have less moral authority, the groups and institutions that offer membership and success will have more influence. When the emphasis is upon status through belonging to groups, it is understandable that conformity will outweigh moral dissent. When the consumer's standpoint in a society of material abundance and great opportunity is dominant, a flexible, self-oriented value strategy is to be expected. Satisfaction with an America that provides such attractive goods and careers is to be expected, for in these terms "we never had it so good." Limited influence of institutions of learning upon student values and character is to be expected when education is sought by the individual as a means of pursuing his life goals, and is supported for its service to the economy and the nation, rather than for its distinctive intellectual and cultural values. The impact of popular forms of culture and entertainment through the mass media of communication has led to a relative decrease in the influence of other institutions and forms of culture. The secular tone of the campus is explicable in terms of the dominant influences of the scientific method, the economy, and the nation. The churches themselves, many students report, provide values more secular than sacred, such as a sense of "belonging" to a unique human fellowship.

4. MORAL EDUCATION IN OUR CHANGING AMERICAN CULTURE

What are the implications of this changing American cultural situation for moral educators? The conclusion is inevitable that what we are now doing in moral education, and religious education as well, is not enough. Either the moral and religious clusters of values are underemphasized, or ineffectively taught, or both. We live in a time when only the most responsible and intelligent, creative and co-operative efforts can preserve our freedom, keep our economy from breakdown, and prevent disastrous nuclear warfare. Our powers over nature and ourselves are increasing; with them come greater obligations. Yet our personal moral standards in such basic matters as honesty, respect for the property of others, and restraint upon the use of violence, and our standards of measurement of national "progress," are evidently declining. Three aspects of this inadequacy in our present moral education are of special importance as negative indicators of what more effective moral education requires:

a. The first concerns the relative importance of moral values today. *The values taught most effectively in our culture will not of themselves make a person or a nation moral.* No civilization was ever as successful as ours in teaching the desirability of participation in the rewards of an impressively productive economy, and the satisfaction of belonging to groups—whether they be clubs, gangs, fraternities, or churches. The values of health, pleasure, romantic love, recreational amusements, individual and family success, comfort and security, progress in economic production and national strength, are all persuasively presented today; and they are all desirable. They are so attractive that persons who are in danger of missing any of them are tempted to disregard, or violate, the moral principles and laws that prescribe the permissible methods of securing life's good things. As Max Lerner points out in *America as a Civilization,* most crimes and disorders "fit the culture."[47] And the characteristic crimes of Americans—whether of delinquents, or criminals, or business and professional people—are against property or for the sake of unjust gain. On the campus the temptations are especially in the areas of personal pleasure and of short cuts to the acquisition of the diploma that makes the values of possession and status accessible.

Moral values are not alone threatened by the dominant influences of our culture. The truth is that all of the clusters of values that have traditionally been considered "higher" are endangered in American life. The distinctive intellectual values emphasized by scholars, the values of pure science, the aesthetic values represented by the most serious and creative artists, as well as the moral and religious values we have been considering, are on the periphery, rather than in the center of American interest and concern. The plight of intellectuals and musicians today illustrates the situation. In a major city the United Fund gave up its support of schools of art and music and of other cultural enterprises because too many donors objected to this use of their gifts. The studies of the campus from which we have drawn were made primarily because there are reasons to doubt that colleges and universities have the influence on student values and character that educators desire. A revision of our previous statement is in order. The values most effectively taught in our culture will not of themselves make a culture *cultured*.

b. *We have no clear understanding as to what persons or institutions are primarily responsible for moral education.* The home, the school, "character-building agencies," the church, the college or university, the service clubs, the government are all involved in moral education. But each institution or group places its primary emphasis elsewhere than in moral education, and expects some other agency to carry the major responsibility for moral training and instruction. No clear lines of division of responsibilities have been drawn; no plans for cooperation in this area formulated. Where responsibilities are not assigned, the work is likely to be half done, or seriously neglected.

Two aspects of this situation are especially noteworthy. The first is that morality is the only area in the clusters of values studied that is unorganized. There are health, recreational, and educational institutions; the family is itself an institution. The economic, political, and religious areas are highly organized. There are learned societies and guilds of artists. Philosophers, scientists, and theologians are internationally organized. But, aside from associations formed to promote certain limited reforms, there is no "Society for the Advancement of Morality." There is no institution specifically formed to promote morality or to support research in it. The second fact is that little specific instruction or training is given to parents and teachers for their responsibilities in moral training and education.

It is almost incredible that the nation which has the most complete educational system in human history gives so little attention to moral education. We have the most inclusive and extensive educational facilities ever available, from the nursery school through graduate schools. We have the most extensive facilities for religious education, with the highest percentage of church members in modern history. We have unprecedented means of communication. Educational television, libraries, and other resources are available. We have the most comfortable and prosperous homes and the most leisure time ever enjoyed. Books by social scientists, philosophers, and theologians give searching analyses of our situation and prescriptions for it. We have the resources of the Western philosophical, religious, and political tradition; the insights of the world's civilizations are available to us. Men and women of great moral courage and wisdom in this century offer inspiring examples to follow. Yet moral education is unsystematic and underemphasized.

c. *Our best-educated young people do not understand the nature and purposes of morality.* They see it as personal and private, rather than as social and imperative. They experience its negative restrictions, but do not understand it as wisdom concerning the way to the fulfillment of human purposes and potentialities. They ask why they should make the sacrifices moral principles involve, and why they should be expected to make social rather than private purposes central in their lives. A much more thoroughgoing interpretation of morality is required, and the appeals for enlistment in the struggle of good against evil will need to be more persuasive. Our society has been preoccupied with external changes—making the world more comfortable and our lives more pleasant. In the resulting process of change, old moral customs have become outmoded and restrictive. Fresh attention needs to be given now to the spirit and purpose of morality, to the basic and enduring motives and principles needed in every age, and to new moral forms in which to express moral purposes in our time.

The following chapters deal with questions raised in this survey of our moral situation. In Chapter II we ask what morality is, what it requires, and what its role in personal and social life should be. In Chapter III we are concerned with methods of moral education, and with the persons and institutions responsible for it. In Chapter IV objections to moralistic education are examined. In Chapter V the religious dimensions of moral education are considered and some conclusions are presented concerning the role of the church in this kind of education.

CHAPTER II

WHAT MORALITY IS

1. MISCONCEPTIONS OF MORALITY

Temptations to do what is wrong and disobedience to moral laws occur in every period of history and in every human life. Our time is not unique in facing serious problems of self-indulgence and dishonesty, delinquency and crime. What is more significant for the future is that so many of us misunderstand the purpose of morality and see its requirements in partial and distorted ways. Effective moral education includes more than prohibitions and exhortation; it interprets the role of morality in personal and social life.

Three fundamental misconceptions of morality are prevalent today, if the evidence presented in Chapter I is reliable and representative. The first is the opinion that morality is a private and personal matter, to be left to the individual person. The second misconception is that morality consists mainly of prohibitions or taboos. It is felt as restraint upon the freedom of individuals and groups and upon the pursuit of happiness and success. It is therefore negatively, rather than positively, related to the goals we seek in our lives. The third misunderstanding is that we are justified in going contrary to personally accepted moral standards when "everybody else is doing it." The conduct of other persons becomes the standard of morality, instead of what is morally right.

Students who interpret morality as personal recognize an important truth. Only persons who judge for themselves and make their own decisions to struggle for good and against evil are ethical in any complete sense. But such persons are mistaken in thinking that morality is a private matter. For the primary fact about morality is its social character. Every human society has a complex moral system. No group of human beings can long endure without a moral code. Gangsters have their own basically antisocial morality, and exemplify genuine virtues, including courage, loyalty, and indomitable, though perverted, purpose. Understandings and agreements are essential to all human enterprises, even when they involve only two persons. "Can two walk together, except they be agreed?"[1] Far greater is the need for unity in large organizations, such as nations.

> Men form a society to the extent to which their lives are ordered by the same morality, custom and law, which jointly constitute the mores of their society.[2]

Three facts about human beings help to explain the inescapability and the social character of morality. First of all, we are gregarious; as Aristotle said, "Man is by nature a political animal."[3] Human influences are necessary in order that a language may be learned and intelligence, conscience, and character may develop. Life in society brings rewards and securities we are unwilling and unable to relinquish. Thomas Hobbes rightly described human existence as it would be without social co-operation: "Continual fear, and danger of violent death; and the life of man, solitary, poor, nasty, brutish, and short."[4]

The second fact is that, unlike the highly organized insect societies of ants and bees, human societies are not regulated by instincts, which operate with a minimum of education and external regulation, or by highly specialized biological "castes" within the society, which are inevitably assigned to food-gathering, defense, or nurture of the young. Human beings must develop their own customs and moralities, and choose their own social roles within limits imposed by sex, social heredity, and government.

Recognition of a third fact is essential to an understanding of morality and moral education. Since nature does not regulate our lives by instinct, and since we are capable of conscious foresight and self-control, much of human conduct is "voluntary." It is under the power of the individual, who has freedom to fulfill or reject the particular obligations imposed upon him by his society. It is because we are thus free that we praise and blame, reward and punish, human conduct considered to be voluntary. Moral education which recognizes this freedom seeks the voluntary decision of each person to accept his duties, and to participate responsibly in the common life.

Each newborn infant is born into a society that already has a morality which is more or less faithfully and adequately represented by the parents and other members of the family and community. Obligations of amazing complexity are in this social heritage, and from the beginning, pressure is placed upon the child to obey. That these duties and regulations are not easily accepted is evident from the anguished and angry cries and tears that mark a baby's career, and the gripes, resentments, and mutinies found in the family, the school, and the wider communities in which we participate. It is also evident in the final appeal to force in the form of police power, when the most necessary rules of conduct are disobeyed. The privileges of social life are gained at the price of agreements to which we are held, of some obligations which we disobey or disregard at the price of punishment, of other duties which we are normally expected to fulfill. What moral education must make clear is the necessity of rules and regulations, tacit and written agreements, laws and codes, in order that the unity and order of society may be established and maintained. Morality is basically neither private nor optional, but social and essential.

Moral education is therefore at once individual and social in its tasks. On the one hand it is primarily concerned with winning the allegiance of the individual. For in the final analysis only freely accepted obligations and purposes are fully moral. This truth was stated negatively by Augustine:

No one does well against his will, even if the thing he does is a good thing to do.[5]

On the other hand, social life requires regulation of human conduct; murder and rape are not made right or tolerable by being in accordance with a man's will. There are requirements so basic that they cannot be left to the discretion—or indiscretion—of individuals. In such matters, where moral education fails, the enforcement agencies of a society must act.

Morality has a protective function in human life. Many of its rules are stated in negative form, such as: "You shall not kill."[6] From the beginning of our lives it restrains us from what we would do if we were left alone. Henri Bergson has described the pressure of society upon us in childhood:

> What a childhood we should have had if only we had been left to do as we pleased! We should have flitted from pleasure to pleasure. But all of a sudden an obstacle arose, neither visible nor tangible: a prohibition. Why did we obey?[7]

As the standards of society, expressed first of all as social pressure to obey, are internalized in the life of the developing child, the inner voice of conscience is more evident in its accusing than in its directing role. Parents and teachers are tempted to place the primary emphasis in moral instruction and exhortation upon the prohibition of conduct that disturbs the peace of the family and the school, or is particularly abhorred. What moral codes are designed to prevent is more evident to a younger generation than what they are intended to foster and achieve. This is the situation today. Our culture encourages strong desires for excitement and pleasure, adventure and thrills, success and popularity. But our rules and instruction in the realm of morality emphasize what is disapproved or forbidden.

Where in our educational process today is morality interpreted in terms of its purposes and of its contributions to the well-being of individual persons and of society? Without such an initiation into the spirit and requirements of morality we cannot reasonably expect young people to devote their lives to the struggle against evils that threaten us, and to the struggle for the preservation and fulfillment of a democratic society. The principles and rules of morality must also be considered, for the individual needs to know what his obligations are. In addition to understanding both its purposes and rules, a third element in a complete interpretation of morality is a description of the characteristics of persons who exemplify the moral life at its best. To these three aspects of the content of moral education we now turn.

2. THE PURPOSE OF MORALITY

If young people are to be initiated into the spirit of morality, and are to understand its purposes before the college years when systematic ethical theories may profitably be studied, popular and vivid ways of presenting it are needed. Morality itself is so complex and so bound up with particular laws and customs, codes and regulations, that analogies are more instructive than direct attempts to summarize and interpret it. What is morality like? Four "models" that might assist the interpreter of morals are: a garden, a game, a family, and a nation.

a. *Morality is like a garden.* R. B. Perry maintained that human life is like a garden, requiring cultivation and containing many different interests and values:

If human life be likened to a garden, then morality and its institutions (conscience, polity, law, and the economy) represent the fencings, spacings, and arrangements by which the plants, such as truth and beauty, and divers special and personal interests, are enabled to flower most abundantly. Morality does not germinate the plants, but makes room for them—for each according to its peculiar requirements. This would have no meaning were there not interests demanding room. To consider morality as

the supreme end in and of itself reflects a profound misunderstanding of its role. Its values are compounded of
other and prior values; its claim to control rests on its
provisions for these values, and for its several forms of
perfection.[8]

The positive purpose of morality is clearly presented in this
analogy. Morality does "space," give opportunity to, and protect the many kinds of goods enjoyed in civilized life. There
are similarities between morality and a garden. But the differences make it gravely defective. For man is not only the
gardener who has developed civilization and who selects,
spaces, and cultivates the goods of life. He is also the chief
threat to his ordered garden. Morality is mainly concerned
with the character and conduct of the gardeners, who are individually inclined to neglect their responsibilities and to
evade their proper share of work, and who are collectively in
danger of destroying the garden and themselves in wars for
mastery of the world.

b. *Morality is like a game.* Morality is more like a game than
a garden. The French novelist Albert Camus said that his only
true lessons in morality came from sports. He described the
moral instruction they provided as "loyal obedience to rules
of the game jointly defined and freely accepted."[9] Both games
and morality regulate human behavior under conditons of
tension and struggle. Both require self-discipline and training.
In both, the admirable person accepts the spirit of the endeavor, manifests a respect for his fellows, insists that the rules
be fairly and strictly obeyed and enforced, and pays tribute to
excellence of achievement on the part of opponents as well as
of his own associates.

Procedures used in training for participation in games have
a bearing upon moral education. Love of the game and desire
for the recognition awarded those who become outstanding
performers lead to willing acceptance of the coaching and the
self-discipline which are essential preparation for skilled per-

formances under the pressure of competition. The rules are accepted because they are neither arbitrary nor negative in purpose. They are designed to resist the peculiar temptations of the particular game, to recognize the limits of human endurance, to encourage teamwork and skill, and to make possible the achievement of the goal by those who deserve to win. Coaching is carried on largely within active participation in the sport itself, and its purpose is positive—the perfection of skills and teamwork. The players are encouraged by applause and recognition, and urged on by cheering spectators. A culture which can generate so much enthusiasm and achievement in sports and games, which are unrelated to the conflicts and achievements that matter most in our life, should be able to improve its training and achievements in morality.

Even the temptations in games and sports are analogous to temptations to become immoral: self-interest—which seeks unjust advantages, emphasis upon winning at any cost, and participation for extrinsic reasons such as financial gain. It is not surprising that athletic scandals and dishonesty in examinations occur on our campuses; both place private gain above moral obligations. It is disturbing that investigations and efforts to correct the situation are more evident concerning the offenses in sports, which are less significant in terms of personal and social consequences, than concerning examinations.

The analogy between a game and morality is useful, but limited in its scope. The spirit of the sportsman who freely accepts rules and discipline is admirable, and essentially moral. But it is found in our amusements, whereas morality is concerned with crucial decisions and outcomes in real life. There is a fundamental immorality in any emphasis upon sports and games which overshadows or adversely affects morality. Morality is concerned with matters of greatest importance: individual responsibility and character, our fundamental relationships with each other, and the future of mankind.

c. *Morality may be compared to a family or a nation.* Analogies from human institutions are familiar elements in our

Judaeo-Christian religious heritage. The family, the most intimate of our institutions, offers distinctive clues to the moral life. In it, persons differing in sex and age are bound together with lifelong ties of affection and concern, and the resources of the group are used to meet the needs of each member. In accepting each member and providing for his development as a person, in establishing relationships of mutual love and helpfulness, in providing secure and satisfying life in community, in readiness of one person to make sacrifices for others, the family is the institution that best exemplifies the spirit of the moral life. It has resources that are not available in wider and more impersonal institutions, for it has its basis in strong natural ties of sexual attraction and romantic love, parental devotion, and biological kinship. Furthermore, its obligations are experienced in face-to-face relationships. There is, therefore, no simple or direct way to extend the moral characteristics of the family to wider communities or to mankind as a whole.

The nation-state offers other clues to the moral life. The nation in Biblical tradition is a model for morality within a religious frame of reference. The concept of the Kingdom of God based upon the analogy of the nation, recognized that the conditions of human life are given, rather than completely subject to our will, and that there is a suprahuman authority that the state should obey. Taken as a human institution, the nation is one of man's greatest achievements. Law and order have been extended over wide geographical areas and include immense populations. Different styles of morality, both personal and social, are found in different cultures, achieving in distinctive ways and in varying degrees fulfillment of such basic moral principles as justice, freedom, and equality before the law. It is significant that the nation too is united not only by laws and customs but also by strong ties of feeling that come to a focus in the complex sentiment of national patriotism. The chief defect in the analogy of the state is that it suggests the enforcement of laws rather than voluntary moral conduct.

The analogies of the family and the nation illustrate the essentially social character of morality. They also indicate that morality depends upon sentiments and loyalties, not upon intellectually discerned principles or commands and prohibitions alone. This does not mean that moral codes and "laws" are unimportant, or that reason has played no part in the extension of morality into larger and larger organized groups: from the family, through the clan, to the modern nation, and to international organizations. It does mean that moral education must be concerned with our loyalties as well as with our principles.

d. *Conclusions concerning the purpose of morality.* An essential task of moral education is to interpret the purpose of morality, and to show why each person should accept its individual and social obligations. There is convincing evidence that we are at present far more effective in presenting the negative principles of our moral codes than we are in explaining what morality is and in presenting its positive goals. The four preceding analogies help us to look beyond particular duties and codes, and to see morality in perspective.

A common element in our four models is that *order is introduced into the relationships between individuals.* In a garden the plants are spaced, fenced, and arranged so they may develop. In a game, rules make order possible within a competitive relationship, in which all may share the pleasures of the activity and some may have the joy of deserved victory. In a family, conflicts are inevitable, but the goal is the unity and security that results from the triumph of love and of morality over divisive motives and conduct. In a nation, law and order are extended over wide areas, and provisions are made for the development of the many values afforded by a complex civilization.

In all four analogies *social order depends upon individual character and responsibility.* Gardeners select plants that are fruitful and useful. "Loyal obedience to rules of the game jointly defined and freely accepted" is only possible where individuals are good sportsmen. One recalcitrant member of the family can prevent the achievement of harmony. Even the nation, which enforces law and order, can endure only if it has a majority of loyal and obedient citizens. Talleyrand is reported to have given this advice to Napoleon: "You can do anything with bayonets, Sire, except sit on them." It is freely accepted moral principles that distinguish morality from compulsion and make ordered institutions possible. The purpose of morality is difficult to state because it is complex.

It is individual persons who exemplify the spirit and purpose of the moral life and who enjoy the values that morality fosters and protects. On the other hand, Kurt Baier is right in his observation that Robinson Crusoe had no need of morality.[10] For it is only in the relationships of a society that human existence, with its obligations and responsibilities as well as its privileges, is possible. *The goal of morality is at once social and individual: an ordered and just society, providing as much freedom as possible for individual persons who accept and fulfill their obligations, and achieving peace so far as this is attainable.*

3. THE RULES OF MORALITY

Every form of morality seeks to regulate human conduct, for some kinds of conduct are better than others. Western movies correctly distinguish between "good guys" and "bad guys," even though in real life the lines of division are seldom so clear or the triumph of good over evil so complete and predictable. Since moral education seeks voluntary self-regulation of his conduct by each member of society, it must include knowledge of our duties, and standards for evaluating motives, intentions, acts, consequences, and character. From the time of Hammurabi and Moses to the present, the duties of men have been formulated in codes and put in memorable form in the Ten Commandments and other summaries of the requirements of morality.

Despite current reactions against "moralism," legalism, and conventionalism, general rules and principles are essential to morality. Good conduct is possible only when a person knows how to distinguish between good and evil, to estimate probable consequences of the various actions open to him in a particular moral situation, and to find the act that is morally the most suitable for him under these unique conditions. Good motives and intentions are essential, but they are not enough; intelligent discrimination between right and wrong, better and worse, is required as well.

The teacher of morals faces difficulties in interpreting the rules and the norms of morality today. Each new philosophical theory presents its own formulation of the goal and the standards of morality. Furthermore, even moralists who share the same philosophical or theological orientation often reach opposite conclusions concerning what is morally right in such matters as euthanasia or the testing and production of nuclear weapons.

There are nevertheless some underlying agreements concerning the areas of human life requiring regulation and the basic obligations that hold for all human beings. Every religion and every enduring philosophical theory includes helpful insights into the human situation and the nature of morality. Many of the rules and standards presented in various moral theories and religious traditions can be restated and combined in orderly and consistent fashion, within the perspective of a moral theory that finds as the purpose of morality the development of the lives of persons within an ordered and just society.

Some of our rules, such as the moral content of the Ten Commandments, express what Kurt Baier calls "moral convictions."[11] They indicate in a positive way certain human goods to be protected: life, the family, property, reputation, etc. Negatively, they call for the restraint and regulation of human drives and desires. William Ernest Hocking summarized the major areas of self-control and social regulation in these words:

Civilization is dependent for its existence not on repression but on the restraint of random impulses, and especially on three restraints—that of the random fight-impulse in the interest of orderly living, that of the random sex-impulse in the interest of the family, and that of the random grab-impulse in the interest of property.[12]

Moral rules of a second type formulate claims that other persons have upon us. They include such duties as being truthful in communication, fulfilling promises and tacit agreements, distributing goods and honors justly, returning favors for favors received, and contributing to the happiness rather than the unhappiness of associates. These are at the same time conditions of the moral health of the community, for they bring open, honest relationships, and protect the welfare of each citizen. The person who fails to meet these obligations excludes himself from the most satisfying human relationships. It is increasingly evident that it is difficult to distinguish between the conditions of moral health and of mental health. Dr. Dana L. Farnsworth, of Harvard University, in addressing an annual meeting of the American Medical Association defined mental health as that "state of mind in which people can carry on their activities with some sense of responsibility to others and without making nuisances of themselves to large numbers of other people."[13]

A third kind of moral teaching offers guidance to the individual who seeks to fulfill his moral potentialities and responsibilities. Some of the rules concern his motives. Love of neighbor as himself, acting to obey the moral law, acting to promote the greatest happiness of the greatest number, or to produce the greatest possible good, or acting so as to become the best possible person in a good society are major formulations of the motives considered best. Here a decision is necessary as to which of these motives most fully expresses the spirit of morality. There are also lists of the virtues that characterize the morally admirable person. These include courage, temperance, wisdom, generosity, humility, and the like. Contemporary ethical thinkers add that the person has responsibilities for his own development. He is obligated to acquire the knowledge and skills needed in his work and in his social responsibilities. C. I. Lewis has formulated two of the imperatives that arise from our human capacities for foresight and for personal integrity.

> Be consistent, in valuation and in thought and action. Be concerned about yourself in the future and on the whole.[14]

A fourth type of moral rule is seldom explicitly stated but is always implied in a culture. In the West, women and children leave a sinking ship first; in traditional China, the men were saved first. Priorities are established according to the ranking of values within a particular society. Kurt Baier has stated the general rules of priority in Western civilization:

> It is generally agreed in our society that moral reasons are superior to reasons of self-interest, reasons of long-range interest superior to reasons of short-range interest, and reasons of self-interest superior to mere pleasure or pain.[15]

While this is a correct interpretation of our moral tradition, our survey of the present situation, in Chapter I, indicated uncertainty precisely at this point of the priority of moral considerations. Explicit consideration of the rules of priority is therefore essential in moral education today.

A fifth type of moral principle summarizes the requirements of morality in one general law. The Golden Rule is the most familiar example: "Whatever you wish that men would do to you, do so to them."[16] Immanuel Kant proposed the formula that we are to act only on maxims that we can at the same time will as universal laws.[17] What the Golden Rule and its philosophical versions mean is that moral requirements hold for everyone alike. It calls attention to a temptation we all experience: to act in ways that are not permissible by the standards we ourselves apply to others. The Golden Rule provides a test of one's own behavior: Is it reversible? If the act I am thinking of doing were directed toward me, would I approve of it? Nonreversible conduct involves us in inconsistency, for we disregard our own standards. It also violates the basic principle of justice, which W. M. Urban defined "as the feeling of moral symmetry."[18]

The sixth and final category of moral rules includes the most general statements of the social goals of morality. "Blessed are the peacemakers" is a commendation of those who contribute to the goal of social harmony. Plato maintained that the supreme goal of individual and social endeavor should be a just society, in which disciplined persons fulfill their varied personal and class roles under the government of those who know what justice requires. The analogy of the family suggests the brotherhood of man as the fulfillment to be sought, while the model of the nation looks toward world order under world government.

Moral rules sum up the duties of men, the kinds of motivation and conduct believed to be good, better, and best, and the goal of just and harmonious relationships between man and man. Each principle and each virtue implies its opposite evil or vice. Study of these standards and of their implications for our own lives in our own time is a way to knowledge of good and evil, and to appropriation of the moral wisdom of the human race. It also is a way to discover for ourselves something that prophets and philosophers have known for many centuries: that the obligations and purposes of morality are universal.

4. THE MORAL PERSON

That systematic and philosophical investigation of morality that we call ethics provides important resources for moral education. An ethical theory interprets the moral life and provides criteria by which choices between right and wrong, good and evil, may be made. However, the most difficult problems in morality and moral education lie elsewhere. Do we want to have our misunderstandings corrected, and to regulate our lives by ethical principles? A grateful student thanked the writer for his instruction in logic. "I had no idea that logic would be so useful," she said. "Through my knowledge of fallacies I was able to get the Honor Board so confused that I escaped a penalty recently." Similarly, knowledge of moral principles may enable the astute practitioner of immoralities to be more successful in escaping social penalties. Good character and experience of the moral life, as Aristotle pointed out, are prerequisites of ethical reflection. The study of ethics will make one wiser, but not necessarily better.

Morally good persons are not only examplars of the ethical life; they are essential to a civilization. Impressive evidence to support this judgment has been published in the journal *Christianity and Crisis* by Langdon B. Gilkey, an American who spent the war years as a prisoner in a Japanese internment camp in the Far East. Food was furnished in inadequate supply to each national group in the camp. When everyone was on a near-starvation diet, kitchen workers were tempted to satisfy the hunger of their families with food stolen from the kitchen. Rumors of dishonesty spread through the camp, but few wanted to be "informers." All enforcement powers were in the hands of the prison guards, and public opinion and moral persuasion proved to be as ineffective in this miniature community as they are in international organizations which also lack police power.

If a man was "posted" on the bulletin board for stealing, he and his friends would merely laugh—why should he care if the "stuffy, respectable hypocrites" thought him wicked?[19]

The community refused to impose limitations upon the privileges of those guilty, presumably since the majority themselves wanted freedom to steal if the opportunity came.

The resulting moral disintegration undermined justice and

order, and revealed the ultimate dependence of government upon morality.

> All of this lit up a striking truth about any community living: namely, that the power of the constitution, the law, or the government of a community is directly proportional to the amount of community responsibility and group feeling that exists there. Coming out of camp, it is interesting to note that many sensible people really feel that a world government can create a world community—in camp we found the cause and effect relationship just reversed; there a declining sense of community responsibility and feeling rendered our constitution and our government almost useless as a force for law and order.

The problem was to find enough honest people to fill the responsible positions where temptations were greatest.

> Thus we came to the conclusion that ultimately the civilization of our community depended solely on the character of the people in it. If the community is spiritually sound, then there will be enough responsible people to fill the important posts. If, however, the community is spiritually unsound, then, as we could see all too clearly, there is no path that that community can take to keep itself from a hopeless anarchy.[20]

This experience of Americans in a concentration camp offers a decisive experiment in which penalties for violation of laws are removed and the economic resources of the community barely sufficient to maintain life. Only the moral character of a minority of persons stood between the group and the anarchical "war of every man, against every man" which Thomas Hobbes called the state of nature.[21] This experiment shows the falsity of the view held today that we are justified in going against personally held or traditionally approved moral standards when "everybody else is doing it." A majority opinion that stealing food at the expense of the lives of other persons should be condoned will neither make the conduct morally right nor protect the particular society from the consequences of its failure to provide the minimum moral basis of confidence and security. It is precisely when the majority have lost their moral bearings that the moral courage and integrity of the minority are most essential. Even if they cannot prevent anarchy, they offer a basis for the re-establishment of civilized order. The direct and immediate purpose of moral education is therefore the training of such persons. A description of their characteristics will indicate some of the more specific purposes of an education that is designed to provide the conditions for the recruitment and development of persons of good character.

The first mark of the moral person is that *fulfillment of the moral obligations summarized in the rules considered above takes precedence* over self-interest, family interest, and the desires of his associates. Unless he possesses this ethical seriousness and purpose, he will be moral only when it is expedient to be so, or when what the group expects of him happens to coincide with the principles and purposes of morality.

Socrates, who refused to give up his mission to improve the moral life of Athens, or to flee into exile when he was ordered by a majority vote to drink the hemlock, accepted the priority of his moral obligations.

> A man who is good for anything ought not to calculate the chance of living or dying; he ought only to consider whether in doing anything he is doing right or wrong— acting the part of a good man or a bad.[22]

He also saw clearly that morality is an essential condition of an economic order; the co-operative production of economic goods is not possible without self-discipline and mutually accepted agreements.

> I tell you that virtue is not given by money, but that from virtue comes money and every other good of men, public as well as private.[23]

Jesus expressed this priority of righteousness over prosperity in theological terms.

But seek first his [God's] kingdom and his righteousness, and all these things [economic goods] shall be yours as well.[24]

A second characteristic is that the moral person can contribute to the order and peace of society because *he takes responsibility for himself* as well as a responsible position in the life of the community. It is not simply that he knows he will be accountable for his decisions and conduct by his fellow men. He displays a self-discipline and inner source of order that reduces to a minimum the needs for external social controls. Henri Bergson observed that "obedience to duty means resistance to self."[25] In many cases, as we have seen, it also means resistance to opinions and pressures from other persons and from groups and institutions. It is evident that such self-discipline does not result from social pressure alone, and that such a sense of social responsibility goes beyond a self-oriented philosophy of life. Morality, and moral education, require a delicate balance between the individual and society. At present our educational procedures center so largely in the individual and his development that his purposes and satisfactions seem to him more important than his obligations and responsibilities.

A third characteristic of moral persons is *sensitivity*. In part this is awareness of the person's own motivations, feelings, and insights. It includes responsiveness to the various elements in each moral situation in which a decision is to be made, and recognition of the most important moral claims and obligations in it. It requires social sensitivity as well. Morality is not in its essence a matter of rules, but of "human-heartedness" (Confucianism), or "compassion" (Buddhism), or "love of one's neighbor as oneself" (Judaism and Christianity). Without this concern for persons, moral principles and rules are impersonal and legalistic, and responsiveness to social expectations means merely conventional morality or equally conformist immorality. Conscience is also a very important aspect of moral sensitivity. Being a conscientious person is an individual matter in the sense that moral insight becomes truly one's own; yet it is not what one pleases but what is morally right and obligatory which is freely accepted.

A fourth characteristic of a moral person is, or should be, *reasonableness*. Only a thoughtful person can be concerned for long-range consequences, understand the moral situation in which he must act, examine the probable consequence of each possible response to a moral situation, and find the appropriate and successful means to implement his decision. A confused student wrote on an examination paper: "Conscience is infallible, but we should not always follow it; sometimes we should use our reason." The truth is rather that neither conscience nor reason is infallible. Yet we must act by the light we have, and seek greater knowledge and insight. The creative solution of the new moral problems mankind faces will require intelligent inventiveness and insight as well as good will.

There are other marks of outstanding representatives of the moral life: vision, humility, courage, determination, and effort. Knowledge of right and wrong, good and evil, brings perspective; it makes possible the vision of a life that would be more ideal. The tension between the ideal and the real, what we are and what we ought to be, sometimes brings fanatical leaders and movements of reform; more often it brings a sense of imperfection and a feeling of humility. Moral education has not completed its task until it inspires effort to overcome evils and to make our common life more just and orderly and meaningful. "To live morally," said A. E. Taylor, "is to live to make the good real."[26]

CHAPTER III

MORAL EDUCATION

1. WHAT MORAL EDUCATION DOES

Moral education is a part of the process of "enculturation" through which each new generation acquires its human heritage and is prepared to assume responsibility for civilization in its turn. It includes the communication of a tradition, with its convictions, principles, and wisdom about life. It is effectively done only if each child learns the attitudes that make such words as "stealing," "honesty," or "fairness" morally significant. It can be called successful only when the obligations of a civilization are understood and responsibility accepted. The ancient Hebrews wisely provided impressive ceremonies in which the members of the twelve tribes renewed their covenant with Yahweh, and the young people joined in public vows of acceptance of political, moral, and religious obligations and loyalties.

Human beings do not become moral *without* training and education. We are potentially moral at birth, but Kurt Baier rightly observes that morality "is our second rather than our first nature."[1] The positive implication of this fact is the necessity of moral training from the earliest days of infancy, and of a moral education that inducts the individual into his heritage and responsibilities. The negative implication is that neglect of moral education in a culture will result in increase of disorder and evil. R. B. Perry stated this aspect of the human situation in philosophical terms:

It is a notorious fact, reluctantly accepted by modern thought, that human individuals if merely permitted or encouraged to grow in accordance with their own innate propensities, will bear evil fruit as well as good.[2] The theological doctrine of original sin goes farther. It adds that the inclination to do evil as well as good acts persists even among those who are encouraged to grow according to the spirit and principles of morality. Undue self-interest will be found in subtle forms in even the most exemplary lives.

Moral education is therefore concerned with the direction of human energies toward social and constructive goals, the development of mature and dependable character, and the enlistment of every person in the struggle for good and against evil. R. B. Perry has ably stated the dual nature of this kind of training. It is at once individual and social:

It is the learner and not the teacher who is the ultimate consumer. He is an end in himself, and he can be reshaped only through his own responses. The fact remains, however, that moral education implies guidance and control —external guidance as a means to inner control. . . .[3]

Moral education so fashions the individual's will as to fit him for participation in the moral institutions—the social conscience, polity, law, and economy. It implants in each individual such dispositions as shall enable him to live and work with others, both *in* the present and *for* the future, and on every level of human interaction and interdependence.[4]

There is a difficulty about education in this field that we ought to recognize. Whether it is successful or not depends in the final analysis upon the response and decision of the learner. While some methods are better than others, use of the best methods of training and instruction known cannot guarantee success. Conformity to social expectations can make a man respectable in conduct, and obedience to law will make his actions legal, but they will not assure us that he acts from good motives, or is capable of distinguishing between good and bad customs and laws. Nor is an easy conscience an assurance of right conduct. A trusted secretary of a building and loan association, known to the writer, systematically robbed depositors and the institution. When his dishonesty came to light, it was found that he had even pocketed deposits of a blind neighbor. Yet after he was imprisoned he said to a friend: "When will you secure my release? I do not belong here with all these crooks."

Acceptance of a religious code or a moral theory is no assurance that moral education has succeeded; many of the most reprehensible acts in human history have been done in the name of religion or morality or both. Fanaticism is a continuing danger among reformers of all kinds, who are tempted to use the most immoral means to the improvement of the world. The unquestioning loyalty sought by nations and other institutions gives support to evil, as well as good, in their policies. Education and culture do not necessarily carry moral sensitivity with them; Heinrich Himmler is reported to have had a beautifully appointed home, filled with the finest books and paintings. Nor can we be sure that any particular method of education will succeed. A strict moral regime in home or school may turn children against morality, while permissiveness is more likely to lead to self-indulgence than to moral seriousness and purpose.

A social scientist states that we probably now have knowledge enough to control the development of a child so that he will become a criminal. Success in such a controlled experiment would be a scientific triumph. Why is it not attempted? For moral reasons. What we may be less likely to recognize is that a scientific experiment designed to produce a saintly person by conditioning and external control would also violate the spirit of morality. For moral education, beyond the period of infancy, involves not only pressure to conform to essential social regulations and moral laws, but an appeal to the mind and conscience of a respected and free human being. There can be no certainty of success, for an appeal can be, and often is, rejected.

2. How Moral Education Is Accomplished

Moral education aims at the development of responsible persons, but it begins before the infant is capable of being responsible. Aristotle described the first stages of the nurture or training that precede formal ethical instruction as "habituation" of the irrational aspects of human nature, which, as he proves, is prior to our rational nature. "The proof is that anger and wishing and desire are implanted in children from their very birth, but reason and understanding are developed as they grow older."[5] Moral virtues arise in us as a result of habit; "we become just by doing just acts." Moral virtues such as good temper are learned by doing them, and "none of the moral virtues arise in us by nature," though we are "adapted by nature to receive them."[6] Since learning good habits provides a basis for good character, and makes us capable of profiting later from instruction in ethics, learning bad habits makes us evil, and unwilling to accept moral instruction when it is given. Both our philosophical and our religious traditions anticipated the modern psychologist's stress upon the importance of our experiences in the earliest years of our lives. "It makes no small difference," said Aristotle, "whether we form habits of one kind or another from our very youth; it makes a great difference, or rather *all* the difference."[7]

Moral training begins in whatever ordered regime is found in the home, in the love that gives security and makes the child's own acts of loving possible, and in the limits increasingly set to the uncontrolled desires and acts of the child. It is carried on in part through explicit commands and prohibitions and imposed restraints, and in part by the examples set by the members of the family and the immediate community. Words and sentences are learned with their emotional overtones and valuational meanings. Subtle expressions of approval and encouragement, and their opposites, influence the child's sensitive nature, and provide him with clues to what is expected of him. Rewards and punishments, praise and blame, acceptance and rejection are forms in which the pressure of society is experienced by the child. It is in response to these human influences that our earliest habits are formed, the content of conscience is learned, and the direction of the development of character is determined.

One of the limits to the direct improvement of moral education is that on this most basic level we influence children largely by what we are, individually and collectively. Moral nurture occurs in the give-and-take of family and community life, and much of the time we are unconscious of the moral influence that we exert. The quality of nurture and training received by a child depends largely upon the character of the persons around him, and the moral climate of the particular time. Philosopher G. T. W. Patrick expressed this truth in terms of his own boyhood experience:

> As a boy I learned three things of priceless value. The first was the duty of absolute truthfulness at all times and under all circumstances; the second was the duty of profound respect for womankind; the third was complete fidelity to any task assigned or undertaken. I do not believe that these principles were learned through any church Sunday school or day school, neither do I recall that my parents ever said anything to me about them. They were simply taken for granted. They were in the social atmosphere.[8]

The social atmosphere has changed, and what is now taken for granted is not preventing the symptoms of moral crisis examined in Chapter I. If it is true that the unconscious moral influence of the family and of the culture is largely what we deserve to have, then the betterment of moral education calls for changes in ourselves and our common life, as well as in methods of training and instruction. That this is not impossible is demonstrated in the history of morals, which includes reform as well as retrogression.

But morality is not taught by indirection alone. Many processes of training and instruction are employed during the years of development "from thinghood to selfhood," to use J. B. Pratt's succinct phrase.[9] These are subject to conscious scrutiny and improvement. Before we turn to some of the most important specific aspects of moral training in the years of childhood and adolescence, consideration of methods in an analogous field with which we are familiar may provide perspective.

Musical education, like moral education, involves both the communication of a tradition and training in ordered action. It begins with conduct and practice, not with the history or theory of music. We acquaint the child with good examples of musical performance; fortunately, excellent compositions have been written for children. While in morality we assume that everyone is an authority, in music the lessons are given by someone especially trained to know what good habits to establish, and what can be taught at each stage of development. The child begins to make music under skilled direction. He is expected to practice so that he acquires skills, which later enable him to give his attention to expressing the spirit and content of a composition. His performances are criticized in the light of accepted norms, and he experiences frustrating failure as well as gratifying achievement. The goal is perfection of performance, both in terms of technique and expression. The best instruction in performance is found in private lessons, continued for many years. For the goal is individual excellence, which is achieved only when the musical tradition is understood, standards made the performer's own, and the person's unique characteristics encouraged—to the extent that they are admirable. Increasingly the learner becomes his own critic, and is capable of interpreting compositions for himself. If he participates in ensemble playing, he engages in unusually sensitive and disciplined social co-operation. If the process of musical education is partially successful, a realm of enjoyment is opened to the pupil, and he gives his support to musicians and to music education. If it is fully successful, a dedicated musician commits himself to a socially useful and creative life. The highest levels of musicianship are achieved through disciplined efforts and sacrifices of other interests rarely found to the same degree in the moral life.

Moral training in many ways presents greater difficulties than those found in music. It must be carried on today by those who do not possess the authority of special training. It is done amidst the tensions and conflicts of family and community life, by those who are emotionally involved and personally concerned. It is usually spasmodic rather than systematic, for no program of graded lessons and of graduated standards of achievement has been developed in morality to compare with procedures used in training musicians.[10] It is therefore important to examine the various aspects of moral training and instruction that might be included in a systematic program.

The goal of training and instruction in the years of childhood and adolescence is the development of character. While habits acquired in childhood contribute to good character, in the final analysis character is not the product of social conditioning and pressure. It is the result of the personal attitudes and decisions that govern the orientation and goals of one's life. The child who is to develop this desirable type of character needs to acquire at least five capabilities, attitudes, and virtues: conscience, respect and sympathy for other persons, reasonableness, responsible self-control, and courage.

Conscience is a unique human capacity through which the

individual responds to his moral obligations and comes to regulate his own conduct. Before conscience appears, parents must assume responsibility for setting limits to the child's conduct, and issuing commands that guide him concerning what is required and expected. Before the child can say "I ought," he responds to commands, "You must." In his first years he has no other source of knowledge of his obligations than his interpretation of what his parents approve and disapprove. It is the parental standards which are the first content of conscience.

In his book entitled *Becoming*, Gordon W. Allport describes the emergence of conscience in a child:

A three-year-old boy awoke at six in the morning and started his noisy play. The father, sleepy-eyed, went to the boy's room and sternly commanded him, "Get back into bed and don't you dare get up until seven o'clock." The boy obeyed. For a few minutes all was quiet, but soon there were strange sounds that led the father again to look into the room. The boy was in bed as ordered; but putting an arm over the edge, he jerked it back in, saying, "Get back in there." Next a leg protruded, only to be roughly retracted with the warning, "You heard what I told you." Finally the boy rolled to the very edge of the bed and then roughly rolled back, sternly warning himself, "Not until seven o'clock!" We could not wish for a clearer instance of interiorizing the father's role as a means to self-control and socialized becoming.

At this stage the external voice of authority is in the process of becoming the internal . . . voice of authority. The parents' task is to enlist the voice in behalf of virtue, as the parents themselves conceive virtue.[11]

Julian Huxley reports that recent studies show the crucial importance of the mother's role in the first three years of the child's life. Children without moral training may grow up as creatures without ethics.[12] Having a good conscience is a matter of being well brought up.

Positive relationships with other persons provide a second basis for the moral life. Children who develop sympathetic and imaginative identification with other persons in their pleasures and pains are unlikely to be guilty of the acts of brutality that are increasingly common now. It is unlikely that such love and respect will develop unless the child receives love from others, and also learns what it means to suffer. In attempting discipline by nonviolent means in our homes and schools we are undertaking an experiment of great moral significance. But it seems doubtful that we have found the moral equivalent of corporal punishment for children who have not learned sympathy for those who suffer, and the concern for others required by the Golden Rule.

A third human capacity that develops only through nurture and training is *reasonableness*. A child needs to learn how to make moral decisions. The mature moral person reflects before making a decision in complex or unusual circumstances, examines the situation in which he is to act, tries to foresee probable consequences of various solutions to the problem, and judges his proposed conduct in the light of moral standards and purposes. Unless the child is trained to use reasonable procedures, he is not likely to act rationally in situations in which thoughtfulness is needed. The point is not that rational analysis is a sufficient basis for morality; we also need the dynamic of motives, sensitive discrimination of values, and attitudes of love and respect for other persons. Nor is it that the human race has yet achieved a high degree of rationality. F. E. Sparshott, a philosopher, recognizes the limits of reason:

> In fact, of course, people do not act reasonably most of the time, nor do they wish to do so; and it is quite obvious that reasoning cannot persuade people to be reasonable, since it is only in so far as they are already reasonable that they will heed the reasoning.[13]

The point is that one will be a more educable and responsible citizen if he is trained to act reasonably as a child.

A fourth central element in a child's moral training is achieved to the extent that he accepts obligations and co-operates with his parents and other teachers; it is *responsible self-control*. Conscience, concern for others, and thoughtfulness are grounds for it. But self-control requires a decision or series of decisions in which the self accepts moral responsibility for itself. Sören Kierkegaard contrasted two stages of life: the aesthetic and the moral. On the aesthetic stage or level the person lives in the present moment; his purpose is to enjoy life, and his principle is: "Live for your pleasure."[14] He seeks out new pleasures, and tries to gain the external resources needed in the search for them, such as money. Because enjoyment is dependent upon factors external to the self, over which we have no control, and because there is a lack of final satisfaction in pleasures, the aesthetic way of life, Kierkegaard maintains, leads to despair. It should be noted that the flexible self-oriented approach to life characteristic of American students today is an expression of the aesthetic rather than of the ethical stage.

The ethical stage rests upon an act of choosing. What is chosen, according to Kierkegaard, is oneself. When I choose myself, I give birth to myself. I "become aware of" the person I am. I take myself, and my responsibility for myself, with complete seriousness. This emphasis upon the self seems essentially egocentric. But Kierkegaard believed that the difference between good and evil becomes clear when we are thus serious and responsible. When we choose ourselves, we cannot ignore our faults and failures, or our relationships to others:

> It requires courage for a man to choose himself; for at the very time when it seems that he isolates himself most thoroughly he is most thoroughly absorbed in the root by which he is connected with the whole. This alarms him, and yet so it must be, for when the passion of freedom is

aroused in him (and it is aroused by the choice, as also it is presupposed in the choice) he chooses himself and fights for the possession of this object as he would for his eternal blessedness; and it is his eternal blessedness. He cannot relinquish anything in this whole, not the most painful, not the hardest to bear, and yet the expression for this fight, for this acquisition is . . . repentance. He repents himself back into himself, back into the family, back into the race, until he finds himself in God. Only on these terms can he choose himself, and he wants no others, for only thus can he absolutely choose himself. What is a man without love?[15]

The most perplexing and difficult problems of the moral life center around oneself. If the self gives the primacy to its own enjoyments and fulfillments, the social responsibilities of the moral life can be but subsidiary and expedient matters. However, if the self simply does what others expect or demand, it does not reach its full stature. Human responsibility is dual— for the development of one's uniqueness, and for the conse- quences of one's decisions in the lives of others. Moral nurture and training should provide the conditions and the encourage- ment for the moral decisions that no person can, or should, make for another. Kierkegaard is right that it takes *courage* to accept oneself, and to become responsible for oneself. It takes courage to join responsibly and freely in the life of groups and institutions, drawing limits to conformity because in- dividuality must be preserved, but also participating in group life because we are morally responsible for the behavior of groups.

The child who does not acquire conscience, concern for others, reasonableness, responsibility for himself, and courage cannot be educated morally. Preaching, exhortation, disap- proval, and appeals to reason are ineffective where these capacities and virtues are lacking. Even punishments fail when persons lack these inner bases of the moral life. For them penalties are resented, and become incentives to greater evil. William Ernest Hocking is right—the state cannot punish:

> For only the man who has enough good in him to feel the justice of the penalty can be punished: the others can only be hurt, or with a finer realism regard themselves as temporary losers in a game which they may try again. The degree of goodness that alone can give a penalty the quality of punishment is something the state cannot compel. To put it crudely, only the good man can be punished. And he would be better without the penalty—he is punished by the judgment.[16]

While these characteristics cannot be produced by compulsion, or guaranteed by even the best methods available, there are a number of conditions that are especially favorable to their development. One of these is a *high standard of achievement effectively exemplified and supported by the family and community in which a child grows up.* We are more likely to do less than is expected of us than we are to do more. And we are not impressed by standards which are proclaimed by people who do not themselves live up to them. Studies of the effects of colleges and universities on student values and character show marked influence only in institutions with distinctive values which students are expected to share. A student's description of his behavior in college is a significant indication of the influence of what Edward D. Eddy, Jr., calls "the level of expectancy" in a community:

> Let me put it this way: where I found weakness, I took advantage of it; but where I found strength, I respected it. If I'm allowed ever to slip by, I'll do it every time. But if I'm really expected to perform, I'll come through or go down fighting.[17]

A second important contribution of a community is *good moral models.* Children identify themselves with those whom they admire, and develop in the direction or directions indicated by acceptable models. The "appeal" of higher levels of character and conduct is greatest when we see them in action. For example, a college professor so honest that he would not applaud an address or performance unless he considered it excellent continues to influence at least one of his students. The contribution of one honest man is incalculable. We have almost limitless resources for moral education in our history and literature, and inspiring examples of moral conduct and courage in our own time. More effective use of them is a way to demonstrate the positive character of morality, and the moral potentialities of the human race.

A third resource that a community should provide for its children and youth is *"coaching" in the form of private and group lessons in the duties and privileges of the moral life.* Aristotle considered a "practically wise man" to be the best source of help when one's own conscience and insight seem inadequate. Parents and teachers have many opportunities for moral guidance, while at the same time giving young people responsibility for the final decision commensurate with the degree of maturity attained. Allowances and the spending of money, the obligations of friendship and of dating, the requirements of education and a career, the ethical factors in vocational decisions, the justifiability of peer group standards, the responsibilities of driving motor cars, and the use of alcohol involve questions of personal and social ethics. In such matters the experience of being held responsible, thoughtful consideration of the justice and injustice of the claims of others, and acceptance of blame for failure as well as praise for success, lead to increasing moral sensitivity and taste, and to self-reliance. Herbert W. Schneider, in *Morals for Mankind,* defines conscience as it develops in firsthand experience as "a combination of a sense of values and a sense of responsibility."[18] The term "coaching" is a better term than "teaching" for the personal instruction needed in morality. It implies correction, expert guidance, and inspiration to courageous performance under pressure.

A fourth desirable resource in a community is *the presence of persons who present goals for life more demanding and satisfying than those now most widely accepted by young people.* Unless life is challenging and serious, moral discipline is experienced as a restriction upon the search for pleasure and success. It is strange that at a time when the disciplined Communist movement is increasing its pressure upon us, when unsolved moral problems of unparalleled complexity and magnitude confront us, and the fate of mankind hangs in the balance, so many young people are preoccupied with immediate pleasures, being "tough," being accepted by their peers, and getting through life as easily as possible. Existentialists who talk of "despair" and "anguish" seem remote from the American scene as we have described it in Chapter I. But they are speaking a language that our statesmen and scientists, our philosophers and theologians can share. It is a sense of the momentousness of moral issues, and of responsibility for one's own destiny and for the destiny of the human race, which must be communicated, whatever the language we use. We need therefore to consider carefully what appeals we can make on behalf of the moral life.

3. WHY WE SHOULD BE MORAL

Two questions occur again and again in the modern world: "Why shouldn't I do what I want to do?" and "Why shouldn't we do what is to our advantage?" They indicate that morality is maintained only against resistance. They also show that human beings are moral creatures at least to the extent that we question our own conduct and seek to justify what we intend to do. Some kind of moral defense is attempted even by the criminal, and by the aggressive nation. There are also more positive forms of these questions: "Why should I accept the obligations of the moral life?" and "Why should we place moral considerations above our collective needs and interests?" We do not give our wholehearted assent to demanding enterprises until we are convinced that we are taking the way to the greatest good. The interpreter of morality must be prepared to answer the questions asked, and to present the strongest appeals that can be made for the moral life.

The lowest level of defense of morality is *the appeal to fear of punishment:* "Do this, or else suffer the consequences." The artificial penalties imposed take the form of corporal punishment, loss of privileges, expulsion from school or loss of a job, fines, and imprisonment. We are unable to protect life and property at present without social sanctions. But when juvenile delinquency costs twenty billions of dollars per year in economic terms—to say nothing of the cost in terms of human suffering; and organized crime is said to be the nation's largest industry, the ineffectiveness of this approach is apparent. While punishment may lead to an understanding of the seriousness of the offense, without more positive appeals the person is more likely to estimate the chances of being caught, and the relative proportions of the rewards and penalties of immoral and illegal conduct. Criminals in a state penitentiary say: "When we are out of prison we live like kings." Punishment alone does not change a person's desires and goals.

The second level of influence is more subtle and more effective. Negatively, it is *social disapproval of conduct that falls below the acceptable level; positively, it is social acceptance.* It is effective when a person desires to be accepted by "respectable" society. It is difficult to overestimate the influence of the human desire to be at home and at ease in the groups one values. If it is a group with high moral standards, one's conduct improves, though motives may remain unchanged. But the need for social acceptance works just as effectively in antisocial groups, such as gangs; it is therefore not in itself a reliable basis for morality.

Beyond this point in the interpretation of morality *appeal is made to its advantages and purposes.* Some of these are egoistic, in the sense that the individual sees personal reasons for acceptance of his duties. "Honesty is the best policy" is a particular formula in which morality is presented as an advantageous way of living. It is true that a moral life normally brings rewards, and that "morality is an uncommonly happy way of living." The disadvantage of the appeal to expediency is that immorality is at times advantageous to its practitioners. The philosophy of expediency does not lead to a firm commitment to duty.

George Bernard Shaw justified honesty in terms at once individual and moral. He answered the question of what you should tell a child who has been caught in a lie, and who does not see why he should be reprimanded:

> You might as well tell it the final truth of the matter, which is that there is a mysterious something in us called a soul, which deliberate wickedness kills, and without which no material gain can make life worth living.[19]

The appeal to personal self-respect and integrity is a valid one, though it is strengthened by recognition of the social context of duties such as that of telling the truth. For not only is the loss of one's soul intolerable; it is also unbearable to conceal the truth from others. The student who wins an essay contest or a degree by hiring a ghost writer cannot enjoy his success, for he is not the person others think he is. What we desire is the security of being accepted as the persons we are.

The social nature of the moral life adds another level of justification and incentive. *Civilized life, in fact any tolerable group life, is possible only for those who fulfill at least the minimum requirements of morality.* The attractiveness of a life that adds to the happiness and welfare of others, and to the order and prosperity of one's nation, can be presented persuasively. For the purpose of morality, which we have expressed as the development of individual persons in an ordered and just society, appeals at once to whatever feelings we have for our fellow human beings, and to our rational natures. Finally, if religion has any place in our lives, the purposes of morality will be seen as ways of fulfilling the will of God for man.

Being moral, as Prof. Donald Walhout has said, "is both mandatory and valuable."[20] The enduring obligations and purposes of the moral life are not arbitrary. They are requirements of civilized life. They both protect and foster life's goods. They express a wisdom about life which a new generation ought not to have to discover for itself through tragic personal and social failures. The most persuasive answers to questions about the justification of morality are positive. Paul wisely wrote to the Corinthians: "I will show you a still more excellent way."[21] Each new generation is asked to test and verify for itself the reasonableness of the duties, and the personal and social benefits, of the moral way of living.

4. Who Is Responsible for Moral Education?

No nation has ever had the resources Americans today possess for moral education. We have a great tradition to share with the rising generation. What is most distinctive in it is challenged and threatened—from within by misuse of freedom and movements for restrictions on intellectual freedom, and from without by totalitarian movements of the left and right. We have educated parents, skilled teachers, unparalleled budgets and educational facilities, and audio-visual machines that offer new possibilities for imaginative and dramatic presentation of events, persons, and issues. We have more insight into the processes of enculturation than ever before; psychologists, sociologists, anthropologists, theologians, philosophers, and educators are investigating even unconscious levels of the response of the person to his family, his culture, and his world. We should be educating morally with greater effectiveness than ever before—but we are not doing so. Methods, content, and institutional resources are at hand, ready if we decide to place more emphasis upon moral training and instruction.

The most perplexing problems today concerning moral education center around two questions. First, who is responsible for training and instructing children in morality? And second, how can we give those who are responsible more adequate training for their tasks? These questions will now be considered; the first has logical and practical priority.

Three possible strategies are open to us. The first is to follow the example of Communist countries, and center responsibility for training citizens in the dominant party and in the government. This involves the attempt to control the influence of family, church, school, the means of communication, the arts, the university, and all other aspects of the society. This is a "totalitarian" and "authoritarian" approach. According to Philip E. Mosely, an authority on Russia, the Kremlin "keeps Ivan in line" by three methods. The first is the use of propaganda to control attitudes and thinking:

> To an extent hardly realized by citizens of a free society, with its clash of views and discordance of voices, the 'New Soviet man,' woman, or child is instructed and warned, praised or browbeaten, by a monolithic and orchestrated propaganda machine. Day and night the Kremlin presses its unrelenting and expensive effort to mold men's minds.[22]

The other two methods are the promise of greater material rewards as a result of hard work and support of the Communist movement, and the threat of repression if the support is not given. This alternative is repugnant, for it involves loss of freedom not only for the individual but also for the family and the other institutions of a society. But we shall escape this fate only if we are successful in preserving the moral bases of individual freedom, national strength, and international order.

The second alternative is to set up a new institution to teach morality and further its purposes. As we have already seen,[23] morality is the one important cluster of values for which no specific institution is responsible. In a sense this is a misleading statement, for R. B. Perry is right in saying that we have four moral institutions: conscience, the economy—which provides for our needs and avoids plunder, the polity or political system, and the law.[24] What we do not have is an institution especially responsible for teaching the basic obligations and principles that should be the content of conscience, and for the training of the men and women of good character who can maintain and improve the morality embodied in social institutions. It may be objected that the church already has these functions. But it does not reach all our citizens; it is divided; its primary concern is with religion; and there are reasons to doubt its present effectiveness in these matters. So there are unmet needs that a new institution or movement might fulfill.

This does not, however, seem to be a feasible plan. We are already overorganized in every community. It is not wise to invest economic resources and executive ability in another enterprise, when schools, health and welfare agencies, colleges and universities, artists, and churches need additional funds and leadership. And the influence of concerned persons should be directed toward moral rather than organizational problems as rapidly as possible.

The third strategy is to make better use of the institutions we have, recognizing that responsibilities for moral training and education in a free society must be shared by the family, the school, the church, social agencies, the government, the law, and the economy. Responsibilities for health are not centralized or regimented, yet we are making progress in health education, in overcoming diseases, and in extending the years of active and enjoyable life. If such co-ordinated activities are possible in improving health, they should be possible in moral education as well. There is, however, a difference that weakens the analogy: there are many professionally trained people in the field of physical and mental health, whereas we do not educate systematically in morality. But if use of the persons and institutions presently available is the only live option, the first step is to investigate the most effective distribution of responsibilities, and the second to consider what additional training to provide.

No substitute for moral training by parents seems desirable in a free society, or possible without destroying family life. The parents who brought a child into being have the most direct responsibility for his training and discipline, and the most intimate and personal opportunities to influence a developing life. The child's basic habits, attitudes, and standards develop in the preschool years. In terms introduced by Sigmund Freud, the "ego," the "super-ego," and the "ego-ideal" develop within the first months and years of the child's life, and until the child becomes capable of self-direction and self-control, parents are responsible for the direction of his development. The family has at its disposal the most effective means of reward and punishment, especially where there is a strong relationship of affection between parents and children. In addition to these direct influences of the family, there is evidence that effective character education by other institutions requires the active support of the home. In the Union College Character Research Project the changes and growth in attitudes observable on the basis of church school classes alone have been compared with cases where the same lessons are taught in both the home and the church. The results show that the home is the central institution in character education. The director of the project, Dr. Ligon, writes:

> We have found measurable evidence of effective character education only in situations in which the home has effectively participated. The home "climate" seems to be the most important element in . . . character education.[25]

At present we are more successful in providing social agencies to strengthen, counteract, or replace the influence of least reliable families than we are in assisting the more responsible parents. Parents need first of all to see where present efforts are inadequate, and to have instruction and training for their responsibilities. Some of the parental concern now evident for the child's status in the community, and his amusements and recreation, could be redirected toward his values and character. A more intellectually demanding and temporally extensive program of education in our schools, and opportunities for teen-agers to make responsible contributions to community life, would help the family at the point of providing leisure-time activities, a need now most acute during the long summer vacation from school. How to strengthen the authority of parents and of society as a whole, within the adolescent subculture, is an unsolved problem; more is required than appeals to individuals and to families.

The school is the second institution of importance in its influence upon the habits and attitudes of the child, and the primary institution in the induction of the child into his cultural heritage. Both the process of learning, and regulated life under authority, involve moral discipline and training in useful work. The school is the first widely representative, systematic institution that the child experiences in a daily routine. It can, and should, offer an ordered, just, and therefore basically moral environment. It represents society in general, requiring citizenship, offering rewards and punishment, providing rules for work and play. Public opinion becomes influential, for the child is subjected to continuous expressions of approval and disapproval from his peers as well as from adults. The obligations of civilized life are accepted or resented and rejected, as children react in their individual ways to the school.

To a high degree the moral influence of the school is the result of its organized life and the discipline of learning. The inclusive nature of the school places limits both upon its training and its instruction in morality. H. S. Broudy has pointed out that the schools are already more severe in their discipline than many families are and than the general community is.[26] In communities that lack homogeneity, a greater variety of educational programs and types of discipline than we now offer seems required to meet the needs both of our children and of our highly diversified economy. Even more complex is the problem of the content of moral instruction, for churches, cultural groups, and families disagree. The result has been a decrease in the moral content of education; one investigator reports that 50 per cent of the content of readers and spellers used in schools in the early days of our country had moral significance, as against 3 per cent today.[27] Yet our literature, history, and daily life offer limitless resources for the interpretation of morality. The ambiguous place of the moral cluster of values in our culture is reflected in our uncertainty about the moral responsibilities of the schools and their curricular content.

Other agencies share in the moral training of children and young people. The churches have an hour or two a week of the time of those who attend. In the background are the enforcement agencies of government. The government is also represented in the discipline of military life, which affects the habits and attitudes of millions of men and some women. "Character-building agencies" are largely devoted to recreation, and to the development of various skills; moral training is usually rather indirect. Undeniably they help to "socialize" the child, and they provide adult leadership. Searching inquiries, comparable to those made of the influence of colleges and universities, should also be undertaken to determine what social agencies and programs are needed alongside schools and churches. A number of types of professionally trained workers also deal with the problems of individuals and families: psychotherapists and social workers, marriage counselors, and the clergy. While they are not specialists in morality or in education, they deal constructively with the moral dimensions of the problems brought to them.

Who is responsible for moral education? It is quite evident that a great many of us are. The truth of the matter is that all of us who have obligations to fulfill and influence to exert are involved in the moral life and in its perpetuation. But some of us are more responsible than others for moral training and instruction, and for whatever improvements in these are now possible. We now turn our attention to the consideration of what can be done by persons most directly responsible.

The most difficult problem is to make changes in the moral training given by parents, especially in the highly important preschool years. For parents influence children primarily through their own values and character. If the moral cluster of values seems to parents less important than the child's pleasures and popularity and success, no changes in techniques of child rearing will make profound changes in the character of the next generation. If parents welcome television, comic books, and other commercial products because they get the attention of the children and keep them quiet and entertained, no effective demands for change in such cultural influences will be forthcoming. What is needed is a movement among parents which will help them to understand their responsibilities in moral nurture and training. The institution that reaches the largest number of them is the church, and its opportunities and resources will be considered in the next chapter.

There are more immediate and controllable resources at hand. An increasing awareness of the inadequacy of moral education is apparent among thoughtful parents. Letters to newspapers concerning cases of juvenile delinquency, expressions of concern in groups of married couples in churches, and the sale of books by social scientists diagnosing our situation are indications of potential support in our communities for improvements in instruction in schools and churches and of potential influence upon the moral convictions of our citizens. A reversal of the trend toward the lowest common denominator in conduct as the standard in morality could take place if means of communication, expression, and united effort are provided on the local level by educators, social workers, the clergy, and other trained leaders.

The neglect of instruction in morality on all levels of our public education—and in many private institutions as well—can be remedied by educators. For morality is not an arbitrary set of requirements. It is involved in all organized life, and expressed in our literature, history, political system, and educational theories. There is a common core of virtues and duties, on which all religious and cultural groups agree. Crane Brinton, of Harvard University, recently restated this area of agreement in *A History of Western Morals:*

> Both as to formal philosophic ethical writing and as to folk notions of ethics incorporated in tradition, codes, aphorisms of folk wisdom, the three or four thousand years of our Western recorded history show an unmistakable constant element. Honesty, loyalty, kindness, self-control, industry, co-operativeness are virtues; lying, treachery, cruelty, self-indulgence, laziness, conspicuous and uncontrolled aggressiveness, and selfishness are vices.[28]

To this list of virtues we need to add the basic moral values of democracy: the dignity and value of the individual, the civic rights and obligations of every citizen, opportunity and justice for all, the use of persuasion and of free elections in reaching decisions, and limits upon the powers of government as well as upon the groups and persons within the nation.

Largely because of the separation of church and state, the two traditionally highest clusters of values—the religious and the moral—are almost missing from the content of American education. If the family and the church carried the responsibilities for these clusters of values adequately, the schools could continue to ignore them. But there is no present indication that the interpretation of morality in terms of the core of virtues and values just described will be done in other institutions, or take place automatically. Teachers therefore need to

be trained in the content and methods of instruction in morality, as well as in methods of discipline. Such instruction is essential for the preparation of young people for their roles as
parents and as citizens.

One of the surprising aspects of our present situation is that
morality has no clear locus in the curriculum of the college or
university. It is by no means clear who is to teach the prospective teachers of morality. Traditionally, philosophy dealt with
morals under its branches named ethics and politics. Meta-
physical accounts of the nature of man and the universe also
included some moral considerations. At present ethics frequently consist of analysis of moral language and impartial
consideration of philosophical theories of morality. From such
a perspective the recommendation of particular ways of living
and the initiation of the person into moral tradition are likely
to be considered matters for religion rather than philosophy.
When we turn to the theologian, we find a strong reaction
against "moralism," and a preoccupation with distinctly theological discussions of ethical teachings. Both the ethical and
the theological approaches are valuable, but hardly what the
teacher needs. Anthropologists and sociologists give descriptive
accounts of morals in various societies, psychologists deal with
the emergence of the superego and the ego-ideal, and with the
reactions of individuals to their society. Historians give accounts of morality through the centuries, and literature includes a wealth of case histories, unsystematized insights into
man and his conduct, and descriptions of utopias—ancient
and modern. Economists, political theorists, lawyers, and
judges deal with various aspects of human motivation, conduct, and government.

Since there are professors of religion who deal with the content of the world's religions, it seems appropriate and advisable
that we should also have professors of morals, including in
"morals" the moral convictions, ideals, and normative evalua-
tions of conduct found in the major philosophies and religions

of mankind. One of their functions would be the organization of the knowledge concerning moral ideals and conduct, past and contemporary, which is now available but compartmentalized in such varied branches of knowledge as anthropology, archaeology, history, jurisprudence, literature, medicine, philosophy, political science, psychology, religion, and sociology. Another task would be the teaching of courses in the history of morals and in ethics planned to meet the needs of varied professional groups in our society whose responsibilities and decisions are of great significance for the future. Among such students would be prospective business executives and labor leaders, clergymen, doctors, jurists, military men, psychotherapists, statesmen, social workers, and teachers. Specialists in education are also needed who will experiment with moral education in the schools along lines already marked out in character education within the church by the Character Research Project to which we have referred previously.[29] By such means, morality can come to have a recognized place in our educational institutions and teachers be prepared to offer graded instruction in our obligations and ideals.

There are limitations upon the effectiveness of the schools as educators for character. One of them we have already recognized: that the child has his basic character formed in the family before he reaches the schools. Many pupils resent both the discipline and the instruction given in schools. Another limitation has been implied: we can only teach in public institutions what almost everyone agrees upon, not the highest reaches of the ethical and religious life. But there is another factor inherent in the school even more serious: pupils learn so much that is evil in schools, in language, attitudes, and conduct. The school mirrors its society, even though the official curriculum screens out what is morally and culturally objectionable in our common life. For example, Max Lerner shows that as children from various social levels attend the same school a process of insulation and separation takes place:

> The schools are at once agencies of class equality . . . and agencies of class conditioning. . . . While there is little sense of class or ethnic difference at the start of schooling, by the time the child has reached ten (fifth grade), he has become "socialized" and his preferences marked. Thus the roots of class superiority and ethnic hatreds lie less in propaganda than in social training through one's peer groups.[30]

We are more successful in inculcating limited moralities than we are in teaching and inspiring "open" or inclusive attitudes and endeavors. Each social class, organization, institution, and nation carries with it both obligations, and limits beyond which the obligations are ineffective. We are more effective in securing adaptation to society as we find it than in inspiring reformers and moral heroes. We are more adept on the lower levels of interpretation of morality and in the use of social pressures through rewards and threats, than in the appeals which have inspired the greatest representatives of the moral life. These higher levels of character and conduct have been associated with religion, and we shall consider the place of religion and the role of the church in moral education in Chapter V.

Contemporary philosophy, psychology, social science, and theology include many references to "moralism" as an objectionable form of morality, and to "moralistic" ways of seeking to influence other persons. In Chapter IV the meanings of these terms, and the significance for moral education of the criticisms expressed by writers who use them, are examined.

CHAPTER IV

"MORALISM" AND
MORAL EDUCATION

1. THE REACTION AGAINST "MORALISM"

A reaction against "moralism" characterizes the contemporary intellectual situation in the Western world. Philosophers, theologians, psychologists, sociologists, social workers, and educators are among those who have joined in this protest. This pervasive movement directly affects persons responsible for education in such institutions as the school, the church, and social agencies; parents, and the general community, are at least indirectly affected by it. It is therefore important to examine this movement, to consider its effects—both constructive and detrimental, and to inquire about its implications for moral education in the future.

In its usual dictionary sense, "moralism" has no objectionable connotations. It means "moral teaching or counsel," or "leading of a moral life as distinguished from a religious life."[1] Today, however, it has become for many persons an opprobrious term. In this current usage, "moralism" refers to moral principles, laws, or customs that have become external and oppressive, and that threaten the genuineness and the creativity of the inner life of the individual person. Since there are a number of intellectual movements that have contributed to the present significance of this term, we shall first consider the sources of the objections to moralism and customary morality. Then the definitions of "moralism" that are important for moral educators will be stated. With this background before us, we will examine the positive and negative emphases of this movement of protest, and their implications for moral education.

The first of the protests against an external conformity to society with its conventions is found in existential philosophy, which as a philosophical movement began with Kierkegaard and Nietzsche. The existentialist objects to conformity to what one's society expects, simply because that is what "one does." He asks for the courage to be oneself, and to remain unique and free. A recent statement of this demand for personal decision and involvement is clear and to the point:

> Through his vacuity, our all too intellectual and technical modern man has fallen, by and large, into a state of unessentiality, mediocrity, lack of genuineness, and alienation of self. He has lost an inward, self-responsible status, has no inner convictions, only repeats what he is told. . . . How easily he succumbs then to propaganda and mass suggestion, until he is finally ready to let a dictatorship make his own decisions for him. . . . The great insight of all philosophy of existence is that it is no good to profess to self-acquired insights, values, and duties, unless this profession has become one's most inward possession through an existential attitude.[2]

From this standpoint, "moralism" threatens the freedom, the responsibility, and the authenticity of the self.

A second major source of the reaction to a merely external morality and to moral exhortation is found in depth psychology. The psychotherapist must avoid a moralistic attitude toward his patient, for, as C. G. Jung says:

> he knows very well that the preaching of even the worthiest precepts only provokes the patient into open hostility or a secret resistance. . . . The psychic situation of the individual is so menaced nowadays by advertisement, propaganda, and other well-meant advice and suggestions

that for once in his life the patient might be offered a relationship that does not repeat the nauseating "you should," "you must," and similar confessions of impotence.[3]

The depth psychologist is concerned also with indications that anxiety arises from a conflict of the superego with the ego and the id, and that an unhealthy repression may result from a rigid and compulsive conscience.

A related influence upon our attitudes toward moral judgments and exhortation is found in the social sciences. The anthropologist seeks to understand each of the world's cultures in its own terms, rather than to make a moralistic approach to them. The social scientist needs the objectivity that is a mark of the scientific attitude, and he is keenly aware of the diversity of moral judgments in various cultures, and even within a given civilization. The social worker, concerned to restore delinquent youth and criminals to life in ordered society, finds that acceptance and trust are more likely to be effective than criticism and moral exhortation.

A fourth major source of the present reaction against moralism is found in Protestant theology. From the apostolic period to the present day Christian thought reflects a tension between "the law of Moses" and "the law of love." The relationships between "law" and "gospel," human effort and divine grace, are perennial themes in Christian theological and ethical literature. The Protestant doctrine of justification by faith rather than by obedience to the law requires a continuing protest against any doctrine that denies the primacy of faith in our relationship to God. Contemporary theology is also strongly influenced by the existential and psychological movements described above.

Another source of the reaction against moralism is found in twentieth-century educational philosophy. John Dewey's objections to "transmissive" education, in which learning is by rote, led to an emphasis upon problem-solving activities in which the ideas and ideals of the past become tools for creative solutions to present problems. In this approach to education, external discipline maintained through external rewards and punishments is expected to be replaced with the freely accepted discipline of co-operative school activities.

Protests against merely conventional morality are also found in various movements among artists, and in their Bohemian colonies. The existentialist's insistence upon personal uniqueness appears in expressionism, and the Freudian emphasis upon the dynamic forces in human nature and their expression in imaginative forms is evident in surrealism. Social realism in the arts leads to the portrayal of moral decay beneath the complacent surface of society. One of the most extreme rejections of society's values occurs among the "beats," who define a "square" as an "unhip conformist." Since "to be hip" means "to know experientially," it is apparent that this is one of the many forms that the search for freedom and authenticity takes in our time.[4]

2. Why "Moralism" Is Considered Objectionable

Objections to moralism have been made from quite diverse perspectives. The philosophers, psychologists, social workers, theologians, educators, and artists we have been considering see quite different dangers to morality or to religion in external conformity or moral exhortation. In order that the implications of these criticisms for moral education may be determined, we need first to see as clearly as possible what the term "moralism" means in each of these varied meanings, and why it is considered objectionable.

The first and simplest definition of "moralism" equates it with "conventionalism" and "legalism." Even when an established order of society is basically moral, there are dangers to the individual in the kind of conformity which Kierkegaard called an "empty externalism."[5] For one thing, since the standards do not really belong to the conformist himself, he does not develop the ethical sensitivity needed for a genuinely moral life. For another, the moral creativity of the individual is lost, and with it the resources for ethical renewal when old forms become outmoded. Furthermore, from the standpoint of the individual, a loss of self-identity occurs. Rollo May has explained this:

> *Compulsive and rigid moralism arises in given persons precisely as a result of a lack of a sense of being.* Rigid moralism is a compensatory mechanism by which the individual persuades himself to take over the external sanctions because he has no fundamental assurance that his own choices have any sanction of their own. . . . If your self-esteem must rest in the long run on social validation, you have, not self-esteem, but a more sophisticated form of social conformity.[6]

From the standpoint of a society, such conforming individuals offer no resistance to totalitarian claims by institutions such as the state. Finally, from the standpoint of religion, complete conformity to one's society is idolatrous, for the social order is given the unconditional obedience which belongs only to God.

A second definition of moralism suggests that it is obedience to an external morality imposed by society through the superego—which is the voice of society within the person, in contrast to the person's own insight and freely accepted standards. This is based upon the discovery of psychotherapists that moralistic condemnation and exhortation is detrimental to the achievement of maturity by the neurotic patient. Conventional morality is therefore more deeply rooted within the personality than is at first apparent. Inner conflicts, guilt feelings, and unhealthy repressions are among the related phenomena reported by depth psychologists. It is believed that similar, though less extreme, results are found in the lives of many "normal" persons today.

One of the results of moralism is a tendency to deny, and even to repress, aspects of the self that are contrary to the superego and the ego-ideal. Dr. Alphonse Maeder, a Swiss psychotherapist, reports the case of a young man who was in despair and in danger of suicide after his discharge from military service. He had been unjustly treated by his superior officer, but he was so conscientious that he denied that he hated the man who had mistreated him. The hatred of another person, which was repressed because of his conscientiousness, turned upon himself. As Dr. Maeder puts it, "Out of a certain decency one hates one's own life instead of the person who has been insulting."[7] A third definition of moralism can now be stated. It is an idealism that results in rejection of aspects of the self that are not in accord with consciously accepted ideals, and consequently issues in self-deceit, since what is rejected cannot be acknowledged.

Paul Tillich calls this state of rejection by the self of aspects of the total self "estrangement" from oneself—since in the experience of guilt the norm of the "essential" self is contradicted and the self is divided. He also calls this state of estrangement from our essential being, "sin." What is needed is "salvation," the theological term for the state of being healed, or made whole.

Tillich sees in psychoanalysis one of the forms of the existentialist movement in the twentieth century. Existentialism protests against the increasing power of consciousness, as against the unconscious and irrational aspects of human nature, in modern industrial society. While there are other forms of the philosophy of consciousness—including the emphasis upon the intellect in the thought of Thomas Aquinas, the Renaissance, and Descartes—he sees a particular significance in Calvinism:

In Calvin it was the moral consciousness, the moral self-controlling center of consciousness that predominated. We have in America, which is mostly dependent on Calvinism and related outlooks, the moralistic and oppressive types of Protestantism which are the result of the complete victory of the philosophy of consciousness in modern Protestantism.[8]

Tillich believes that the psychoanalytic movement, with its emphasis upon acceptance of those who are unacceptable and upon the recognition of aspects of ourselves that have been denied or repressed, lends support to the recovery in theology of the doctrines of forgiveness, grace, and reconciliation.

A fourth definition of moralism is that it is a moral idealism which becomes divisive and inhumane as its adherents seek negatively to avoid disloyalty or compromise, and positively to make their ideals dominant in the world. John Dillenberger points to the social disunity that such idealistic movements produce:

> The moral man has a system of values, ideas, and hopes which he always sets between himself and others. As a result, the very things he believes in divide him from others and make impossible communication and above all an element of charity and love.[9]

Reinhold Niebuhr stresses the inhumanity that results from the idealist's failure to see that his purposes cannot be fully realized:

> Moralism may be defined as a form of morality that holds to moral norms without recognizing that in actual history these norms always confront recalcitrance and without knowing that every moral norm is part of a whole web of moral means and ends. These norms are not, therefore, as simply realizable as the idealist imagines. It is the complicity of this web that makes moral prudence one of the virtues of political morality, and frequently the supreme virtue.[10]

A fifth definition of moralism is found in the criticisms made by Protestant theologians and religious educators of much of the preaching and teaching in Protestant churches. A foreign visitor to American churches, impressed by much that he saw, expressed his concern about the sermons he heard. "As far as I can ascertain," he said, "the paradigm of American preaching is 'Let me suggest that you try to be good!' " Such preaching is in danger of reducing religion to morality; as Dean Inge once said, "The gospel is good news, not good advice." Both the difficulty of the Christian life, and the contrast between Christian teachings and the life we live, are ignored in the moralistic preaching that Reinhold Niebuhr has defined and opposed:

> This moralism, which consists in holding up the high ideals of brotherhood and love to men and nations on the supposition that nothing more than their continued re-iteration will ultimately effect their realization, is a disease of the American church.[11]

He quotes from Kierkegaard to show that in such preaching and teaching a sense of contrition and a recognition of the power of self-love is missing:

> A minister who preaches the love commandment without also revealing how desperately difficult if not impossible it is to love the neighbor as himself, proves thereby that he has never taken the commandment seriously or sought to apply it in his own life.[12]

This power of self-love means that we do not succeed fully in living by the law of love even in our personal lives. In social terms "there is no known specific justice which is not also in-justice when viewed from the perspective of the love command-ment." Moralistic preaching "does not realize that even if all men professed Christ and even if they understood his gospel so well that they felt under the tension of the commandment,

'Thou shalt love thy neighbor as thyself,'[13] the fact of sin would still make political and economic coercion for the establishment of justice necessary." Professor Niebuhr adds that moralistic preaching assumes that forgiveness of others is a direct moral possibility, instead of a by-product of religious tension in which the person recognizes his own need for forgiveness. What is unique in the church is not the preaching of ideals:

> If there are not notes of judgment and mercy, of contrition and grace in the preaching of the church, its message is not only futile but confusing. For religion must deal with the total dimension of human life and not with the surface of morals. If that surface is to be dealt with alone, it is better to allow secularists to deal with it. At least they will not add religious confusion to moral superficiality.[14]

A sixth definition of moralism that is relevant to moral education is that moralism "makes virtue in the self, rather than the good toward which a virtuous life is directed, the object of its concern."[15] An example of this turning of virtue in upon itself is found in an interpretation sometimes given of Jesus' teaching in the Sermon on the Mount, in which the Mosaic commandments forbidding the acts of murder and adultery are extended to include the motives of anger and lust. The context from which such teachings concerning motives are interpreted should include the other-regarding character of Christian love, with its concern for the consequences of our deeds in the lives of others. When the context of love's solicitude for the neighbor is omitted, the objective and social differences between evil *motives* such as anger and lust, and the evil *acts* of murder and adultery, are overlooked. This is moralistic in the sense that "virtue in the self rather than the good toward which a virtuous life is directed" has become the center of ethical concern.

The seventh definition, and the final one to be considered, is that any form of morality or any moral system that is interpreted as self-sufficient or self-authenticating is moralistic; for then what is good and evil is judged apart from God's self-revelation. This objection to moralism is made from a position such as that of Karl Barth, who separates theological ethics sharply from philosophical ethical systems and from secular morality. Christians, Barth said recently, should not act according to rigid moral principles, but only according to what Christian faith tells them is God's will in Jesus Christ. "Christians should be free," he said, "to give an attenuated Yes or No—according to circumstances—whenever an absolute categorical position is expected of them and a categorical Yes or No whenever no such stand is being asked for." The Christian should consider himself free to "say Yes today when he said No yesterday."[16] In part this is because the Christian's ultimate commitment is not to finite persons and institutions, and in part because the Christian should not deny to God freedom to act in a new and creative way in human history. But it also reflects a rejection of secular morality.

3. Positive and Negative Aspects of the Reaction Against "Moralism"

The objections raised against moralism, defined in various ways, are among the many symptoms that something is wrong in our present moral and religious life. They are based upon valid insights that educators should take into account in seeking effective ways of teaching morality and religion in our changing culture and world. Since protests always include negative elements, and are usually one-sided, a critical examination of these criticisms is needed also. We shall look first at the positive contributions of the movement that has been described in the first two sections of this chapter, and then at its adverse effects upon the moral life of our time.

First of all, *it is true that morality can be dangerous—*though it is also true that immorality and amorality are even more dangerous. Morality can be misused—just as religion, philosophy, science, and all other aspects of human culture can be abused. Morality can lead to a self-righteousness that conceals the failures of the self or the group, while the pretensions of others are clearly recognized. It sometimes leads people to be more concerned with their own idealism than with the good that they might accomplish for others. It can lead to fanatical movements which seek to impose a moral and political system upon others, and which use evil means to reach the desired goal. Yet self-righteousness and fanaticism are perversions of morality, not essential ingredients in it, or necessary results of the moral life.

A second important insight is that *social conformity does not in itself produce a moral person.* External discipline and institutional authority are not in themselves adequate means of moral training. Paul Tillich has stated the need for inner and individual moral resources:

> External imposition is not sufficient for the creation of a moral system. It must be internalized. Only a system which is internalized is safe.[17]

However, this does not mean that people necessarily desire the responsibility of making their own decisions, or are easily persuaded to undertake the self-discipline and the social obligations of the moral man. What many people prefer is conformity to what Prof. Morton White, of Harvard, has called "a dreary system of ethical rules."[18]

A third insight is that *moral ideals meet resistance both within the self and within society.* We are tempted to identify ourselves with the norms we profess, and to overlook the discrepancies between the ideal and the real. This is closely related to a fourth truth, that *guilt is a universal human problem,* whether consciously recognized or not. Theology and depth psychology find this true not only because all of us share in the failures of our society, but also because each of us experiences an alienation from aspects of ourselves that resist the discipline and claims of morality. Estrangement from self, from other persons, and from God is not adequately met by moral exhortation. The courage to accept ourselves and to acknowledge our individual and collective guilt is needed.

The fifth insight involves another level of life, and approach to reality: *religion is more than morality, though it is relevant to the moral situation.* While religions include difficult and demanding ethical requirements, they offer enthusiasm and power, and a way of salvation that brings forgiveness, healing, and a reorientation of life. The moralistic exhorter misunderstands both religion and the human situation.

A sixth point is made by psychotherapists, social workers, and theologians: *moral exhortation is of limited effectiveness in restoring persons to mental and moral health.* If a person already accepts his moral obligations and needs only to be urged to continue his efforts to fulfill them, exhortation is appropriate. But it does not produce self-understanding on the part of the neurotic, or a willing response on the part of delinquents and criminals, or moral renewal in our churches.

A seventh positive emphasis of those who object to moralism is that *outmoded customs and laws and social forms become oppressive and external.* It is understandable that many people should identify the customs and laws of the past with the essence of morality. What is required in a time of rapid change is a recovery of the spirit and purposes of morality, and a knowledge of its enduring principles, so that morality may be expressed in new forms suitable to the needs and aspirations of the time. There are ways in which Karl Barth's insistence upon freedom to say No tomorrow to what we accept today is compatible *with morality,* though it seems to go farther and to involve the freedom of the religious man *from morality* and not simply from moralism. The moral obligations of the Christian will be given further consideration in the concluding section of this chapter.

The objections that are made to moralism are not, in intention at least, objections to morality. "Moralism" has become a term expressing criticism of external or complacent or repressive forms of morality, and criticism of ways of furthering morality that alienate those most in need of healing and help. Theologians who separate Christian teachings sharply from secular moral systems seek to protect the sources and the quality of the Christian life. The basic insights and intentions expressed in the movements of protest against moralism are constructive in the sense that more mature, humane, creative, and Christian forms of morality and moral education are recommended and sought.

However, the effects of these objections to moralism include reactions against morality itself, even though these were neither foreseen nor intended by the scientists, philosophers, and theologians who have been the leaders in this movement. There is a risk involved in taking the word "moralism," which in its conventional meanings includes the whole realm of morality, to refer only to objectionable aspects and forms of morality and moral education. The result may be, in the popular mind at least, a reaction against the entire extension of the previously accepted meanings of the term. There is evidence that such a reaction against morality, which goes far beyond the meanings of "moralism" as they are given in thoughtful discussions of the problem, has taken place in our time.

Morality today is largely understood in negative terms, as repressive; this is not unrelated to the popular understanding of the implications of Freudian psychology. The failure of the churches to have the expected moral influence as people have turned to them is directly related to the theological protests against moralism, as well as to the moralistic preaching that induced them. A philosopher of education has expressed his reaction to the theological emphasis upon the dangers of our virtues:

Some modern clergymen preach so ardently against "righteousness" that one may be inclined to tell them that virtue
is not necessarily a vice.[19]

And a psychologist calls attention to the curious situation that
results when the clergy accept a psychological interpretation in
which we are "sick" instead of "sinful," and give up the essentially moral nature of human existence:

> How very strange and inverted our present situation . . .
> is! Traditionally clergymen have worried about the
> world's entertainments and entertainers and, for a time
> at least, about psychology and psychologists. Now, ironi-
> cally, the entertainers and psychologists are *worrying
> about the clergymen.*[20]

*The central moral problem of our time is not that of intro-
ducing humaneness into a rigid morality. It is rather that of
teaching the basic spirit and purpose of morality, and the
standards by which good and evil can be recognized.* For people
are now asking why they should accept the claims and responsibilities of the moral life as individuals, as groups, as
nations, and how they can distinguish between good and
evil. It is true that our devotion to duty often leads to evil
consequences. But this is not because we are dutiful, but because our loyalties and the purposes of our institutions are so
limited and conflicting. It is true that many persons need to be
saved from immoral and amoral lives and that exhortation
will not accomplish the change; but this situation is an indication of our failures in moral nurture and education, and
of the subsidiary status of moral and religious values in our
culture. *No movements of protest against moralism, or against
immorality, meet the central moral need of our time. That
need is for positive moral education.*

4. Moral Education and Criticisms of "Moralism"

Educators are responsible for teaching the human cultural
heritage to each new generation. In no realm are the problems

today greater than in morality. Moral education takes place in a cultural situation in which large numbers of persons consider moral values less important than social status and economic success. It is carried on by persons inadequately trained in ethics and the history of morals. Therefore, an increased emphasis upon moral nurture and training of the customary type may not have the intended results. The protests against moralism warn of dangers, past and future. They remind us that some prevalent forms of moral training and of morality endanger the fullest development and unity of the self and of society. They call our attention to this question: *How can we educate for the moral life without being moralistic in the objectionable sense of the term?*

One characteristic of moral education which is carried on in awareness of the danger of moralism is that *its goal is the training of persons who freely accept their moral responsibilities.* External conformity, social pressure, and mass organization neglect the inner sources of conscience, moral purpose, and character. The extreme in the collectivist direction is the mass man, who follows the party line. The extreme in the existentialist direction is a romantic individualism in which the person is authentic and self-directing, but more concerned with his freedom than with the welfare of society. Ours is a highly organized society, under pressure from a still more centralized and disciplined movement—Communism. Our morality, political system, and religion are being tested: can we provide the nurture and inspiration for responsible, moral persons who are capable of co-operation with a minimum of pressure and enforcement from public opinion and government? In the final analysis this kind of moral education rests upon the intrinsic worth of our tradition and goals, and an appeal to the minds, consciences, and loyalties of respected, free, and socially-responsible individual persons.

A second characteristic of nonmoralistic education is that *it seeks to avoid harsh and condemnatory attitudes and punishments which alienate persons from the life of organized so-*

ciety. Educators, clergymen, social workers, and law enforcement officers face a difficult problem in dealing with persons involved in antisocial behavior, for they are expected to be at once sympathetic counselors, and upholders of the claims of society. One extreme response is an acceptance of the guilty person that fails to indicate the seriousness of the offense or to protect other persons from its repetition. The opposite error is the harsh treatment that led a reformed criminal to ask, "What's wrong with the right people?" The situation after a major violation of the requirements of morality is an occasion for moral education or re-education. But the opportunity is lost if the offender learns that moral offenses are not taken seriously, and may be repeated with impunity.

In Chapter I, reference was made to the case of Betty, a student in a school of education who defended her act of representing reports copied from another student as her own.[21] While many students today say that Betty should not be punished because she thought she was doing right, the offense was a serious matter. A prospective teacher was publicly defending dishonesty. One of two things was involved: either she was one of the rare persons who is incapable of distinguishing between right and wrong—in which case she should not be permitted to teach, or she was bluffing—and if her bluff was successful, she would continue her dishonest conduct. The university in which she was enrolled had the responsibility of protecting society against a prospective teacher who refused to admit that dishonesty is wrong, and also of upholding its own integrity. When Betty was expelled from the school of education by the disciplinary board, she admitted that she had known all along that her behavior was wrong, and that the penalty was just. The experience was educational because it did not condone what is morally wrong, and the university, in the light of Betty's changed attitudes, was able to help her find a worthy career in a field other than education.

A third element in a moral education which is planned to

avoid the dangers of moralism is *a fundamental honesty and realism about ourselves and our moral situation.* Emil Brunner has made an observation that is of importance to the educator:

> I suppose everyone makes the distinction between good and evil—with that amazing precision which shows itself especially in criticism of others.[22]

This is true of groups and nations as well as of individuals. Unhealthy repression of the drives and creative energies of the self may occur when we refuse to acknowledge our personal sins. The problems of life in the family and in wider communities become difficult when individuals assume that other persons are responsible for all the difficulties of human life. Peace within and between nations becomes impossible when all causes of economic, political, and international strife are ascribed to our opponents. The possibility of peaceful and freely accepted moral reform rests upon the recognition of the need for it. The moral resources of standards by which to judge self and society, the rational resources of intellectual honesty and the effort to achieve an objective view of ourselves, and the religious resources of humility and love, are needed in the struggle against repressive and fanatical forms of morality.

A fourth implication of the protests against moralism for moral education concerns the churches. The evidence presented in Chapter I concerning the college campus and American culture indicates that all religious groups face problems concerning the relevance and effectiveness of their moral teachings. However, the criticisms of moralistic preaching examined in this chapter were made by Protestant theologians, and the following paragraphs about nonmoralistic moral education in the church also express a Protestant Christian point of view.

Christian morality and religion are theocentric. God is at once the ultimate Being, the object of our highest devotion and loyalty, and the final authority concerning good and evil, right and wrong. The Christian is committed to an objective search for what God asks and requires of us. The final criterion of good and evil is to be found, not in a philosophical search for the highest good, but in God's self-revelation to man. In Christianity this is found in a Person, Jesus Christ, rather than in a code of laws or an ethical formula.

The first thing to be noted about Christian moral teaching is that the Christian stands under much more difficult obligations than does a naturalistic humanist, or a theist who believes that the requirements of religion are within the limits of human achievement. The Christian is to love God with all his heart, mind, soul, and strength, and his neighbor as Jesus Christ loved his fellow man. The final standard of the moral life is divine rather than human. "You . . . must be perfect, as your heavenly Father is perfect,"[23] said Jesus. Prof. John Knox, in *The Ethic of Jesus in the Teaching of the Church,* recently summarized the obligations of the Christian, and the humility that should result from understanding and accepting them:

> We are, in a word, to be perfect as God is perfect. Jesus never dilutes the righteous demands of God or adjusts them to our moral capacities. On the contrary, he presses every moral requirement to its extreme limit. The commandment against murder becomes a prohibition against hatred; the commandment against adultery becomes a prohibition of lust. Jesus reveals little, if any, interest in questions of moral casuistry—that is, questions of what should be done in circumstances where, as we see it, the perfect thing is too difficult, if indeed it is not, as things are, impossible. . . . The requirement under which we stand is not of such kind that any man could ever conceivably discharge it—"No one is good but God alone," he says (Mark 10:18)—but we stand under it nevertheless, and no excuse is tolerable. To be sure, God is ready to

forgive us freely and to the uttermost—but not to exon-
erate us. All possibility of self-righteous complacency or
boasting is shut out.[24]

Since Christians accept obligations that go even beyond our
human moral capacities, more is to be expected of them than
of non-Christians in motive, character, and conduct. This does
not mean that the moral achievements of the Christian are
the basis of his "justification" or acceptance by God. The
doctrine of justification by faith is nonmoralistic in the sense
that God's forgiveness and grace are offered to those who re-
spond in faith, but moral in the sense that a new relationship
of obedient faith and love to God results in love for man and a
transformed life. A religion offers more than moral teachings,
for it includes a way of salvation from evil. The Christian salvation is complex, and includes repentance—or turning away
from evil, forgiveness received—and extended to one's fellow
human beings; reconciliation to God and man; restitution for
wrongs done; acceptance of the goal of a Christlike life in the
service of God and man; and the experience of grace as enthusiasm and power. *Without moral seriousness and relevance,
a religion becomes sentimental and loses its influence. For
then no need for penitence and forgiveness is recognized, and
participation in the organized life of a church makes no
marked difference in values, character, and conduct. But moral
seriousness apart from the religious way of transforming human lives replaces religion with ethics, and leads to what the
theologian calls "moralism" in the preaching and teaching of
the churches.*

While the Christian is obligated to go beyond such basic
moral requirements as honesty, temperance, courage, and justice, he stands under these obligations as do others. Religion
requires a fundamental sincerity and honesty in belief, in facing individual and collective guilt, in relationships to God and
man. Robert Ulich, in *Philosophy of Education*, finds a rea-

son for the declining influence of the churches today at the point of genuineness of belief, though he recognizes the historic role of the church in ethics and education:

> Nevertheless, the tragic fact remains—reminding us of the end of Antiquity—that millions of Christians profess what they no longer believe. For them Christianity has become nothing but a respectable convention which they do not leave because they are mentally too indifferent or because they do not know where to go. This is an essentially dishonest and hypocritical posture, especially dangerous in view of the fact that on the other side of the fence there is now an opponent with a fervent faith and belief in the future—Communism, with its so-called "scientific" dialectical materialism.[25]

The sins of passion and intemperance, as well as those of selfishness and pride, are clearly proscribed in the New Testament. The Christian, who is to obey God rather than men, requires courage. Most of the churches do not advocate elimination of the structures in the economy, the state, and international relations through which justice and order are sought. Justice in both personal and social relationships is a continuing Christian concern, even though love requires sacrificial service which goes beyond what justice requires. The Christian citizen is responsibly involved in the procedures used in his nation for seeking just and peaceful solutions of the conflicts that are found in all areas of organized life, from the family to the United Nations. It is to be expected, therefore, that moral education in the churches will strengthen commitment to universally recognized moral obligations as well as teach the distinctively Christian virtues and duties.

The theological criticism of moralistic preaching and teaching is intended to recall the church to its religious message, resources, and life. Religion includes more than a sense of duty; it is concerned with our ultimate beliefs, values, and devotion. The highest levels of morality and of faith come as a gift rather than as achievements reached by our own unaided efforts. They appear when our lives are transformed by what we admire and love, worship and serve. Religious faith carries obligations with it, but it begins in a disclosure or "revelation" of God and of the highest human excellence, which wins our faith and love. It is concerned with the fundamental goodness of our loyalties and purposes, the ultimate orientation and direction of our lives. A sentence from Augustine indicates how intimately the religious and moral dimensions of life are related:

> For when there is a question as to whether a man is good, one does not ask what he believes, or what he hopes, but what he loves.[26]

Religious faith and devotion, when genuine and focal, have observable moral results. "You will know them by their fruits," said Jesus; the lives of Christians test the reality and character of their faith.[27]

We have found it necessary to consider some aspects of the relationships between religion and morality in this chapter. The movement of opposition to moralism includes prominent theologians, and influences the teaching of morality in the churches. The more general questions concerning the role of religion and the churches in moral education remain to be considered in the following, and concluding, chapter.

CHAPTER V

RELIGION, THE CHURCH, AND MORAL EDUCATION

1. RELIGION, MORALITY, AND THE CHURCH

No serious investigation of morality and of moral education can ignore the historical relationship between morals and religions. The world's distinctive ways of living, admired types of character, and cultural patterns have developed within its religions. Buddhism, Confucianism, Hinduism, and Islam are distinctive in their moralities as well as in their philosophies and forms of worship. Our own tradition is complex, including the Greek heritage of Dionysian and Apollonian types of character and religion as well as the Judaic and Christian.

It is true not only that religion and morals have never been dissociated in recorded human history.[1] It is also the case today that the only powerful rivals of the traditional religions are embodied in humanistic faiths. Communism presents its moral teachings for individuals and societies within its complex structure of beliefs about the universe and man, its convictions about the dialectical process of history, its optimistic promises for the future, and its dynamic "missionary" movement. Naturalistic humanism in its democratic Western forms is also taking the form of a faith, and is seeking converts. Where traditional moral standards and religious faith are becoming dissociated from life, as we found to be the case on the college campus today, it is more probable that a new form of interrelated morality and religion is in the making than that morality and religion are now going separate ways.

The norms and ideals of morality are not independent

factors in a culture. The particular duties recognized vary with the changing conditions of our common life. The specific expectations connected with bank accounts, credit cards, or use of television in political campaigns are understandable only within our present institutional arrangements. But the ways in which we fulfill or evade these social obligations express our central convictions, purposes, and loyalties. The moral life of the individual person as well as of a culture expresses a style of life, a way of living, a response to life as a whole. If it is more than a merely external conformity to customs and laws, the moral life cannot be dissociated from what we believe about the nature of the universe and ourselves, from what we are most serious about, from what we feel to be really good and evil. And these are religious matters. Two very important implications for moral education follow from this inherent connection between morals and religion.

The first inference has been clearly and explicitly made by a writer who expects "from the future that to an ever-increasing extent scientific knowledge . . . will control life and the conduct of men,"[2] and who therefore uses the term "religion" in the broad sense which includes humanistic systems of belief. In his book *Positivism,* Prof. Richard von Mises presents his views concerning ethics and religion.

> Those who study without prejudice the historical course of events will recognize that the present state of moral conduct in almost all countries of the earth was developed under the essential influence of various religious systems. . . .
> *The practically most efficient form of dispersion of ethical doctrines is their incorporation in the framework of religious systems.*[3]

Whether or not we accept a form of a traditional religion, what we need to share and to teach is more than customs and laws and rules: it is an inclusive interpretation of life and our response to it, within which morality "makes sense," and is accepted as a part of a life worthy to be lived by a human being.

The second implication for moral education concerns the church; it follows from what has already been said when it is considered within the distinctive institutional arrangements of our society. One of the contributions of the Christian religion to Western civilization was the development of an independent institution that seeks to be universal. Prof. George H. Sabine expressed in his book *A History of Political Theory* the judgment that the rise of the Christian church

> as a distinct institution entitled to govern the spiritual concerns of mankind in independence of the state, may not unreasonably be described as the most revolutionary event in the history of Western Europe, in respect both to politics and to political philosophy.[4]

It is not that Christianity involved a great change in the attitude toward political rulers, for it has stressed the obligation of civil obedience. It is rather that man's highest duty is to God and not to man, and is expressed through an independent institution. Western man has acknowledged two loyalties: to God, and to the state.

Professor Sabine saw that this independence of church from state contributed to the development of freedom, and changed the relationship of the state to morality and religion.

> It is hard to imagine that liberty could have played the part it did in European political thought, if ethical and religious institutions had not been conceived to be broadly independent of, and superior in importance to, the state and legal enforcement.[5]

The state has given rights to individuals because they were believed to owe an obligation, and to have a destiny, outside the political sphere. At the same time what the government, and the schools it supports, undertakes in moral education is limited. The American doctrine of separation of church and state, someone has said, means that the state is concerned only with second-rate matters. The truth of this analysis is strongly supported by the attacks all totalitarian movements make upon churches, and upon the religious doctrine that man's obligation to God outranks his political allegiance.

The two implications of the inherent relationship between morality and religion for moral education may now be considered together. The first one is that we cannot teach morality effectively apart from our convictions about the universe and ourselves, the purposes that make life meaningful, and the loyalties that we ask children and young people to share. The second is that in our society these ultimate convictions and loyalties are more than political, and are assigned to an independent institution: the church, or to equivalent societies of those who do not find traditional forms of religion acceptable. To make the state responsible for this kind of instruction and appeal would, in our pluralistic culture, limit this kind of education to the level of the lowest common moral and religious denominator. In the long run it would, in all probability, lead to totalitarian nationalism or an equally totalitarian internationalism. The churches are the most effective institutional bulwarks against the tendency of the state to dominate all aspects of human life, and religious beliefs and loyalties are the ultimate resources of the individual against the authority and claims of his nation.

The churches have, therefore, an indispensable role in moral education. They are ultimately custodians of our moral tradition because that is a part of a wider religious tradition: the convictions, purposes, and loyalties through which we interpret human life and relate ourselves to other persons and to whatever power or powers we depend upon for our existence and the fulfillment of our hopes. Thoughtful college students who express a sense of need for religion are reaching out for this inclusive and ultimate interpretation of life.

But if the churches have an indispensable contribution to make in moral education, they must fulfill their role or be replaced by other agencies. Today representatives of the churches themselves recognize that their moral influence is declining. An analysis of the reasons for their present lack of effectiveness is needed before we consider the moral resources of religious institutions and their more effective use. Although the author is a Protestant Christan and assumes that children attend public or secular private schools, he believes that much of the content of the pages that follow is relevant to the situation of churches that support parochial schools.

2. Why Doesn't Increasing Church Membership Bring Moral Renewal?

Churches in America are prospering. The proportion of church members in our population is higher than ever before; over 60 per cent of our citizens are listed on church rolls, and attendance at church services is higher than in any other nation in the Western world. Yet the evidences of personal and social ethical renewal that have accompanied such movements in the past are not apparent. A newspaper headline concerning a report of the National Council of Churches was clear and to the point: "Church Membership Increases; Morality Declines." The churches have a great opportunity to influence our beliefs, our attitudes, and our conduct. But if the campus is a clue to our situation, the effort the churches are now making is not preventing a moral revolution toward a self-oriented life in which moral standards are accepted from the groups to which the individual belongs, and a religious revolution in which secular values rather than sacred ones are sought in the church.

A number of factors in this moral and religious situation bear upon our investigation of the role of religion and the church in moral education. The first is that for some centuries the churches have not had the dominant influence on the development of our culture. Machiavelli, writing in sixteenth-century Italy, presented his theory of the autonomous state which is the first example in modern times of a realm of life that claims complete freedom from moral and religious control.

> A prince should . . . have no other aim or thought, nor take up any other thing for his study, but war and its organization and discipline, for that is the only art that is necessary to one who commands.[6]

The ruler's only concern with morality is that it must be inculcated in his subjects to enforce social unity. This is a power philosophy of pragmatic expediency in which morality is relative to the interests recognized by the ruler. Such a nation-state relies on force in its external relationships, and bends religion and morality to the ends of power within the state. National patriotism has increasingly displaced universal religion as the loyalty around which communities are formed.

Other areas, too, have proclaimed their independence of morality and religion. One of them is the modern economic order which, as John Bennett once said, "grew up when the church was asleep."[7] Researchers at Michigan State University came to the conclusion that the typical business executive has two sets of ethical principles—one for the world of business and the other for his home and church. "The study indicates that ambitious business executives do not regard as success-contributing those practices ordinarily regarded as good human relations," says the study director, Dr. E. E. Jennings.[8] A very important aspect of this independence is that many executives of the movie industry, television and radio companies, and publishing houses decide the content of their programs and publications, so influential in our lives, on the basis of what is successful in commercial terms.

The result is declining influence on the part of the churches, and of the other institutions that we count upon for moral education. C. Wright Mills, in *The Power Elite*, describes our situation.

Families and churches and schools adapt to modern life; governments and armies and corporations shape it; and, as they do they turn these lesser institutions into means for their ends.[9]

Mills gives as an example of the use of religious institutions for ends other than those of religion the contributions of chaplains to military morale, and therefore to effectiveness in killing. Except to the extent that the churches are responsible for their own loss of influence by past and present policies, and willingly accept their subservient status, it is unfair to blame them for what they are powerless to accomplish. It is evident that no simple changes in technique of moral education will change the situation.

A second factor that limits the moral influence of the churches is that the return to churches here and around the world seems to be more largely connected with nationalism and traditionalism than with a search for moral guidance or religious faith. Will Herberg, Graduate Professor of Judaic Studies and Social Philosophy at Drew University, has studied the sociological background of the combination of a notable turn to religion at the same time that our thinking is increasingly secular. American society has been the melting pot in which people of diverse backgrounds have become one people, with three branches of "American" religion: Protestant, Catholic, and Jewish. These religious communities give "self-identification and social location" to Americans, so that it has become

virtually mandatory for the American to place himself in one or another of these groups. It is not external pressure but inner necessity that compels him. For being a Protestant, a Catholic, or a Jew is understood as the specific way, and increasingly perhaps the only way, of being an American and locating oneself in American society.[10]

In a recent article Professor Herberg designates the mass movement into the churches as "the sociological revival of religion as belonging."[11] It is encouraging that he finds evidences of a much more personal moral and religious quest among some thoughtful young people, especially on college campuses and in suburban areas.

To the extent that joining a church is a way of being an American, and therefore of expressing the American democratic faith in its twentieth-century form, the security and preservation of our nation and its culture are sought in our churches. Our traditional forms of religious faith are interpreted from the context of the culture, and profoundly modified in the process. Sydney E. Ahlstrom has given a theological analysis of the American culture-religion of today.

In more recent years a kind of "Christianity of Main Street" has come into being, and with it an implicit theology—a farrago of sentimentality, moralism, democracy, free enterprise, laicism, "confident living," and utilitarian concern for success.[12]

The prophetic and transforming functions of religion are seriously handicapped, if not nullified, when the nation and its culture, rather than the will of God, are the center of concern.

A third explanation of the limited effectiveness of churches today in moral education is found in the dominant concerns of the churches themselves. For one thing, they have been preoccupied with the problems of expansion and growth. These include provision of new churches in suburban areas, larger buildings for the activities of growing numbers of members, promotion of financial campaigns, and measurement of success in terms of membership and the marks of prosperity. In such a time, the institution tends to become an end in itself. An extensive study of church families, reported in *Families in the Church: A Protestant Survey,* found evidence that both laymen and ministers take an institutional view of the church.

Nearly half the parents had avoided any theological reference when they spoke about their faith and church life. For them, something designated as "fellowship" was often lifted out as the chief value. Yet this fellowship was nearer to a modern definition of sociality than to the *koinōnia* of the New Testament.[13]

One result of this institutional focus is that the church becomes a busy world of its own, and the lives of its members are devoted to serving the institution instead of serving God in daily life. The parents interviewed in the survey just referred to

> speak of being caught in a veritable beehive of activity, all aimed at nurturing the organization instead of ministering to the world. That they are not alone in such a caricature can be seen in the results of the questionnaire returned by pastors. . . . Over half of the pastors reflected an opinion that parents in the church owed institutional participation, loyalty, and support above any other expectations. Parents were hardly inaccurate in their supposition that organizational efficiency is what most pastors want.[14]

Another result is that the church becomes another group demanding and training "organization men." The authors of *What College Students Think* found that students who are active church members are more likely than other students to see a moral issue in cheating, but also more likely to cheat when other people are doing so.[15] Participation in institutional life is not in itself the moral training that the world expects from the church, and reliance upon institutionalism accentuates what religion should prevent: the tendency to go along with what others are doing.

A fourth factor limiting the influence of the churches is that neither the theologians nor the parish ministers have found a way to communicate the Christian message tellingly in the present moral and religious situation. In the words of Paul Tillich,

> The reason for the irrelevance of the Christian ministry in our time is that it has not learned to speak to the

people of a largely secularized world in such a way that they feel: this message concerns us ultimately; it is a matter of "to be or not to be."[16]

The result is an unreality in the teaching of the traditional commandment and ideals. They are not rejected; but they do not seem to fit our world. And even if we accept them intellectually we do not see much that we can do to put them into practice.

3. Religion, the Church, and Moral Education

What can we and should we expect of our churches and of religion today? The situation is perplexing indeed when the churches are prosperous and well attended, but when the moral influence expected of a renewed interest in religion is not evident. Prof. Pitirim A. Sorokin, of Harvard University, made a study of seventy-three converts of popular American and British evangelists:

> We wanted to know if the conversion of these seventy-three persons had changed their minds and, particularly, their overt behavior in altruistic directions, by making it nearer to the sublime precepts of the Sermon on the Mount? The result was not cheerful. Out of these seventy-three persons, only one has shown a tangible change of his personality and overt behavior. About one-half of the converts changed somewhat their speech reactions: instead of profanities they more frequently began to pronounce the name of "Our Lord Jesus Christ" and so on, but their outward behavior did not change at all, and the remaining half of the converts did not change even their speech reactions.[17]

Neither the customary church school classes nor the traditional church services and revivals have the moral effects that accompanied them in previous periods of our history.

The moral and religious situation is revolutionary, from the standpoint of both the moral and the religious traditions—which, as we have seen, are intimately related. The moral and religious clusters of values are not rejected, but they have a "ghostly" character. Other factors—science, the economy, the nation—have more influence upon our desires and our choices. Morally we are moving in the direction of self-oriented lives with group standards having the greatest authority. Religiously, church membership is a way of identifying oneself as an American; for many, the experience of belonging to a unique human fellowship outweighs the sacred values of religion. Yet there is a sense of need for a religious orientation and there are mystical aspects of membership in a church, which indicate a point of contact for a profound interpretation of religious faith. In a revolutionary situation, doing more of what we are already doing is not enough, even though it may be one of the things needful. The issues must be met directly and persuasively.

When people are "converts" to a religion in terms of institutional affiliation and personal identification, without evident changes in character and conduct, that religion has lost its authority. Moral education within a religion has a different character than the discipline and instruction of a school. A religion is concerned with the convictions that are central in our lives, the loyalty that takes precedence over every other loyalty, the interpretation of life's meaning and purpose that gives it direction. A. E. Taylor put the point clearly:

> It is of the very nature of a living religion to claim the supreme direction of effort and action. If the claim is disallowed, religion itself ceases to be real; if it is allowed, it is idle to dispute the right of religion to be made the foundation of education.[18]

A religion inevitably includes a morality, for it is an appeal to accept a way of living that expresses one's faith and devotion. Different religions, and variant forms of a particular religion, have their distinctive types of character and ways of fulfilling moral obligations. This is one reason why no general courses in religion can take the place of the communication of a religious faith in its entirety with all the resources of a church—liturgical, theological, devotional, and instructional. A church that does not claim the central direction of the development of character is a church in name only. And, since nature does not guide human lives by instinct, some other group or institution will take over the functions of churches unless they regain their power to influence us at our deepest levels.

It is difficult to say whether a church should begin its appeal with its ethical requirements or with its faith in God. A conversation is said to have taken place one morning between a Protestant minister and a Roman Catholic priest. They discussed their work as clergymen. Said the Protestant minister, "My job is to make good people religious." The priest replied, "My job is to make religious people good." Since we are religious at least in the sense that we seek something to which we can devote ourselves, and since churches start with us in our imperfection and offer ways of salvation, the remark attributed to the priest is a more profound interpretation of the contribution that the church can make.

But there is also truth in the other approach. For we are not likely to take seriously any religion more demanding than the popular cults of personal success or nationalism unless we are ethically serious as well. Sören Kierkegaard placed the religious stage of life *after* the ethical stage. The aesthetic stage, in which life's pleasures are the goal, leads to a despair in which the person takes himself with complete seriousness. Then he becomes aware of his imperfections and guilt. And this sense of sinfulness is a condition, he maintained, to entrance into the Christian life, to the acceptance of forgiveness and to the readiness "to be transformed into likeness with God."[19]

These are conditions of effective moral influence by a religion in any period of human history. There are also some specific needs of our time that can be stated in the light of the preceding chapters of this book. *The first of these needs is training in what it means to be religious.* We teach *about* religion in the church school and in most of our colleges and universities. Even in our theological seminaries we are chiefly concerned with courses about theology, the Bible, worship, and pastoral theology. Much that is done in church schools is not even instruction about religion; it is moral exhortation to live up to conventional standards. Instruction about religion and exhortation to live a moral life are not enough.

We know that studying about science will not produce first-rate scientists. Schools and colleges train students *in* science. They provide laboratories, and skilled instructors who help their students to learn the methods, share the spirit, become excited about the prospects, and accept the discipline of the scientist. Religious training is much more intellectualized and formalized than training in science today. While Hinduism differs in important ways from Judaism and Christianity—placing the emphasis upon achieving a distinctive kind of mystical experience, it is nevertheless appropriate to ask whether anything in our religious training compares with the period a Hindu boy spends as a disciple of a guru, or religious teacher.

Unless we know what it means to be religious, and share in the reverence and awe and self-dedication that mark the religious attitude, the practices of religion lose their value. The term "God" has religious meaning only when it is used by a religious person. It is quite possible to study about religion in church schools, participate in public worship, repeat creeds and prayers, hear preaching, and still be quite secular in one's attitudes and values. The requirements of training *in* religious faith and devotion in a secular age have yet to be explored and met.

A second requirement is one of which theologians are well aware. *It is training in seeing our culture in the light of religious faith.* What the studies of college students, reported in

Chapter I, show is that our American culture has the major influence upon us today. College students think very much alike everywhere in this country. It does not make a great deal of difference in their thinking whether they are Protestant or Catholic or Jew, whether they went to a public or private or parochial school, whether they are male or female, or whether they are white or colored in skin. Our culture, with its immense power through the television and radio, newspapers and magazines, movies, and billboards, has a deep influence upon what we value, what we desire, and what we seek.

What the church seeks to do is to bring the wisdom and illumination of faith to bear upon the problems presented by our culture. But when a secular culture is the chief influence upon values and character, the process is reversed. It is, of course, impossible to see the beliefs and requirements of a traditional religion with other than our own peculiar twentieth-century American assumptions and values. But it *is* possible to have our assumptions and values changed in the light of an honest search for understanding and truth. The scientist looks at facts from the standpoint of existing hypotheses and assumptions. But when the facts no longer fit the theory, the difficult and creative formation of a new hypothesis is called for. An example is also at hand in religion in our time. Christians in East Germany and other Communist countries—who are more aware than most Americans of the difference between Christianity and contemporary cultures—are engaging in searching study of the Bible, and in theological reflection. Johannes Hamel, pastor in East Germany, writes:

Living within the Marxist world, can we understand the stories, psalms, prophecies, parables, and letters of the Bible in any other way than as being directly addressed to the church in this world? In fact, God's Word has assumed a strange straightforwardness. . . . The thick walls of nineteen hundred years have come down. Nothing stands between us and the Biblical Word.[20]

When a culture is transforming a religion, those who seek to understand both their religious faith and their culture need this kind of objective, searching study of their faith and its its contemporary relevance.

A third need is for much clearer guidance concerning what what is good and what is evil. Our inherited commandments are largely negative, and concerned with personal sins. Opinions concerning what is right and wrong are changing rapidly. Attitudes of many churches toward dancing, use of alcoholic beverages, the theater, and other matters of personal morality have changed in recent years. On the other hand, practices such as segregation of minority groups which were socially sanctioned are now condemned in social pronouncements issued by churches. In the morality taught in our churches, is everything relative, or are there abiding criteria of right and wrong? If there are ways of determining what is good and evil, right and wrong, they should be stated as explicitly as possible for the guidance of those who must make the decisions that will determine the fate of mankind.

It would be quite misleading to suggest that the churches need to clarify their teachings concerning good and evil primarily for those outside the churches. One of the most evident facts about the present situation is a widespread disappointment with the churches because their teachings and the human lives inspired by those teachings are so discrepant. A professor of theology, Joseph Sittler, places the contrast between the ethical obligations and the conduct of Christians in historical perspective.

Men set about being "ethical" under the impact and continuing power of the Gospels, within the tutorial structure of the church, and in the light of those ordered presentations of obligation called Moral Theology. And on the way they burn witches; fight wars out of mixed purposes which they persuade themselves are not mixed at all; use venerable and holy names to designate institutions and

practices which they dare not criticize, lest they threaten
worldly securities; pose, posture, lie, and generally per-
vert the organic unity of the life of faith.[21]

It is not enough, however, to answer the criticisms of the moral
effectiveness of the church by pointing to evidences of the
sinfulness of man, and by stressing the doctrine of forgiveness
of sin. We do not even seek forgiveness until we are aware of
our need for it. Moreover, the "church militant" seeks to overcome evil, not merely to forgive the guilty. Christian ethics is
an essential aspect of Christian teaching.

*A fourth contribution that we can ask of churches is training
in analysis of the sources of evil in our lives.* One conclusion
to be drawn from our study of American culture is that much
of our trouble comes not from malevolence but from errors in
valuation. The values stressed in American life are not evil.
We cannot live without economic goods, and success is desirable. Many Americans, however, place a disproportionate
emphasis upon such values, which are essential as "foundations" or "footings" for the distinctively human values, but
are subsidiary, and in themselves incomplete. When the desire
to possess an automobile takes precedence over ethical considerations, crime and delinquency result. It has been said that
the illusions of youth are that sex is love, and that success is
happiness.[22] These mistakes in valuation lead to unrealistic
expectations, and to disillusionment. As H. Richard Niebuhr
has said, "the great source of evil in life is the absolutizing of
the relative."[23] This error in judgment is difficult to avoid. We
can only see what is relative in the light of what is absolute,
what is lower in relation to what is higher, and what is less
good in comparison with what is better. A rich and complex
civilization is in especial need of wisdom in ordering its values
and its obligations. The teachings of the churches can be made
vital and relevant, for religion is especially concerned with
what is of supreme value and importance and with life's
priorities.

If "the absolutizing of the relative" is the most important cause of distortion in our value judgments and of evil in our lives, a second major source of evil is the choice of wrong or ineffective means of seeking good ends. This mistake in judgment is not limited to the Communists who use the method of dictatorship with the intention of moving to a classless society of perfect justice and peace. Man's search for international order has thus far been repeatedly frustrated. This is, in part, because the methods of establishing peace have not yet been clearly formulated or widely agreed upon.

The attitudes and purposes that divide mankind and produce injustice and war are a third cause of evil in our world. There is no assurance that the means to peace will be used, when found, without something more fundamental: the overcoming of hatred and an increase in our concern for mankind as a whole. Religion is especially concerned with changing our attitudes towards other people and overcoming our selfishness and pride, by helping us to become as concerned for our neighbor's welfare as our own. It seeks to direct our energies toward reconciliation, brotherhood, and peace. This is doubtless why Gabriel Marcel, contemporary French philosopher, came to the "unconquerable conviction that, as long as Christianity remained true to itself, Christianity could be the only authentic peacemaker."[24]

A fourth source of evil is that our loyalties limit the scope of the obligations we accept. While the teachings of our religious faiths are universal, extending to all mankind, our loyalties are particular and local. What is good in itself as far as it goes—family, religious denomination, geographical region, or nation—becomes a rival of religion as a source of moral obligation, and limits the effectiveness of religious faith in bringing reconciliation and peace. Repeatedly, in our study of the American cultural situation we have found evidences of an "American democratic faith" which tends to limit our understanding of our religious tradition, and the range of the obligations we recognize. The wisdom of the Biblical tradition in placing the religious commandments of love and obedience to God first, and the moral obligations to one's neighbors second, is apparent. For only an inclusive and ultimate loyalty can sustain an all-embracing morality.

A fifth need today that churches should endeavor to meet concerns the way of living to be recommended to young people. The moral revolution to which the life of the college campus points is self-oriented yet group-conforming.[25] Both these ways have their attractiveness and appeal. In a difficult and dangerous time it seems sensible to look out for one's own interests and seek whatever security for self and family our nation and world afford. In a time when life is highly organized, and even religion seems to be largely a matter of belonging to a distinctive group and institution, the goods to be gained by adjusting to group requirements are more evident than those to be gained in nonconformity. What the church needs to show is both the limitations and frustrations inherent in these ways of life, and also a nobler way of living.

The egocentric and the group-conforming ways of life are in uneasy tension. Either self-love or loyalty to one or more groups will come to predominate, though in our highly organized existence a person may take different attitudes in different groups. If self-interest is dominant over other interests the person is incapable of true friendship, love, loyalty, and devotion. He exploits other persons and groups for his own benefit. Morality is perverted, for the person cannot accept any moral appeal beyond what is expedient to him. And all that he can seek in religion is some resource or advantage for himself—which is the reverse of religious devotion. Self-interest shuts a person out from the experiences that make life deeply satisfying. "For whoever would save his life will lose it."[26]

If group loyalty accompanies group conformity, then, without an ultimate commitment, the person is controlled by his society. He is moral in the sense of contributing to its organized life, but he is involved in the immoralities of our collective life. And unless he has standards by which to judge his society, and the courage to try to reform it where it is wrong, he loses his freedom, his dignity, and his sense of integrity. The final result of this group-conforming way of life is a totalitarian society, in which there is no way of distinguishing good policies from those that are evil. "The man of duty," Dietrich Bonhoeffer wrote, "will end by having to fulfill his obligation even to the devil." But he did not mean that this is true of the man whose ultimate responsibility is to God, who is ready "for the bold stroke of the deed which is done on one's own free responsibility, the only kind of deed which can strike at the heart of evil and overcome it."[27] Bonhoeffer was executed in 1945 for his religious and political opposition to the Nazi government of his own nation.

The sixth condition of effective moral influence by a religion is that responsibility to God must take precedence over other obligations. And this occurs only when devotion to God outranks our dedication to finite persons, institutions, and movements. The most important difference between morality and religion is that morality is concerned with our responsibilities to each other, while religion includes heights and depths of vision, reverence, penitence, unreserved commitment, and hope which are appropriate only in response to what is ultimate in goodness and in being.

The central religious issues of our time come to their focus in the doctrine of God, and in the relationship between God and man. Totalitarian powers object to forms of religion that teach that "we must obey God rather than men."[28] For this means that the nation is judged by supranational standards, and a limit drawn to obedience to its dictates. Totalitarianism makes religious claims, for it seeks unquestioning loyalty, and the central direction of the character and conduct of its citizens. No realistic and farsighted program of religious education in our time will neglect preparation of young people for this continuing struggle against ultimate claims by political movements—including the possibility of American forms of it, whether to the left or the right in political orientation.

Within the free world, forms of religion that center in belief in God are challenged by humanistic beliefs that center in man. Christian ethical teachings are often accepted where Christian theology is not. The result is that naturalistic humanism is not a phenomenon of the secular intellectual world alone. The university professor who called himself "an atheistic Christian" would find like-minded companionship in many churches which profess traditional creeds. When many students say that what they look for in religion is "a focus for personal adjustment and development," "intellectual clarity," and "a strong community feeling of closeness with your fellow man," rather than God, worship, and salvation, the religious revolution from a divine to a human center is observably in process.[29] This is the opposite of a Copernican revolution, for man and this world become the center of reference and faith.

The ethical dimensions of this revolutionary situation in religion are twofold. On the one hand there is the problem of the sincerity of our acceptance of traditional beliefs. The problem of the reality of God, and the truth of our beliefs about him, is inescapable. This is one of the most important issues for religious leaders, especially in dealing with the college and adult age groups within and outside the churches. But on the other hand, there are ethical grounds for religious belief. That moral discipline is a preparation for religious vision is a teaching of the great religions. This is evident in the New Testament. "Blessed are the pure in heart, for they shall see God."[30] The connection between love of God and love of man is inherent: "For he who does not love his brother whom he has seen, cannot love God whom he has not seen."[31] And doing is one way to knowing. According to the Gospel of John, Jesus said, "My teaching is not mine, but his who sent me; if any man's will is to do his will, he shall know whether the teaching is from God or whether I am speaking on my own authority."[32]

It is a significant fact that both religious humanists and theists find the central contribution of religion to be vision—and in particular the vision of God. For the humanist it is man's vision of God which incorporates our highest ideals and aspirations and inspires our noblest deeds and endeavors. For the theist, it is God's self-revelation which brings our answering faith, humility, obedience, and love. Revelation is the center of religious concern for the theologian, the minister, and all who look beyond the claims and interests of the self, the economy, and the nation.

4. THE ROLE OF THE CHURCH IN MORAL EDUCATION

The role of the church in moral education depends in part upon the place of religion in our lives. If religion claims "the supreme direction of effort and action,"[33] then it seems that the church should take full responsibility for moral education, and accept the blame when crises and failures occur. This solution would please many parents, and some public school authorities as well. The uncertainties of the present situation would be ended; and home, school, and church would have distinctive functions.

But the role of the church depends also upon the nature of human development, the resources of our institutions, and the moral nurture and instruction needed in our complex civilization. We must ask what we can reasonably expect of our churches. And a distinction must at once be made between churches that provide parochial schools and those that do not. Parochial schools combine functions that are otherwise divided between schools and churches, but they do not fundamentally modify the situation with regard to the family. The following paragraphs assume the situation in which churches function alongside secular schools.

Three factors are of basic importance in assessing the responsibilities of the church in moral education. The first is the time available. The church has—with considerable irregularity—from an hour to three hours per week of the time of children and young people. Not all of this is available for instruction, and a religion must teach much besides its ethics. The school has thirty or more hours per week, with, of course, a constantly increasing body of knowledge to teach. The family has up to sixty hours per week of the child's time, excluding the time spent at church and school and in sleep. The limits of the educational opportunities of the church in comparison with the family and the school are evident. The result is that the church has fewer opportunities for individual guidance and instruction than do the parents.

The second factor is that the church can do far less in establishing a disciplined regime, and inculcating the habits and attitudes required in citizenship than the school can do with its large professionally trained staff and its daily activities. It is also true that a great deal of the content of the moral life concerns our public activities in the polity and the economy, and our duty under the law, and that this part of moral education properly belongs in public schools.

The third factor is that the church—as does the school—has its opportunity to influence developing human lives *after* the basic habits, attitudes, and content of conscience have been acquired in the family. No other institution can take the place of the family unless it removes the children from parental influence in the very important first five years of a child's life. The influence of the parents is of great significance in religion as well as in morality. Modern psychology has verified the religious character of the child's dependence upon and attitudes toward his parents. Those who reject the Freudian interpretation of belief in God as a wishful projection of the father image are not likely to deny that the images of its parents are the child's chief symbolic resource for the interpretation of God.

It is also true that the sense of the reality, or unreality, of

God comes first through the family. John Baillie, Scotch theologian, recognized that "God's earliest disclosure of his reality to my infant soul was mediated to me by the words and deeds of my Christian parents." His description of the role of the family in his own religious and moral development, given in his book *Our Knowledge of God*, suggests that much of our present difficulty comes from a change in the life of the family:

> No matter how far back I go, no matter by what effort of memory I attempt to reach the virgin soil of childish innocence, I cannot get back to an atheistic mentality. As little can I reach a day when I was conscious of myself but not of God as I can reach a day when I was conscious of myself but not of other human beings. My earliest memories have a definitely religious atmosphere. . . . I cannot remember a time when I did not already feel, in some dim way, that I was "not my own" to do with as I pleased, but was claimed by a higher power which had authority over me. You may say that this higher power represented only my parents or my nurse. If by this you mean that that is *your* view of the source from which the claim proceeded, then I am not for the moment concerned to refute it. But if you mean that that was *my* view of the matter, then I must dissent. For, as far back as I can remember anything, I was somehow aware that my parents lived under the same kind of authority as that which, through them, was communicated to me. I could see that my parents too behaved as though they, *even they,* were not their own and might do what they liked and might ask of me merely what they liked to ask, or their authority over me could not have had the character which I actually felt it to possess. No, with the best will in the world, I cannot say that it was the social organism to which I belonged that seemed to be claiming me. Rather was I a member of a social organism that was itself aware of a claim.[34]

The significance of what Professor Baillie says about his childhood is not only that the family inevitably teaches religion or irreligion in the earliest years of our lives. It is also that his parents *had moral authority* because they had a tradition to teach, and exemplified in their own lives the responsibilities to God and man which they expected their children to accept. They had something to teach the next generation, as well as a faith to live by. And if the church were to accept full responsibility for teaching morality and religion, it would thereby indicate its willingness to see the family deprived of its spiritual functions, as well as to see the moral and religious nurture and training of children neglected until after the foundations of character and conscience have been acquired.

In a little-known essay on "Youth and Authority," Prof. Eugen Rosenstock-Huessy shows that the migration of immigrants from many religious groups presented such educational problems for Americans that in 1850 they turned decisively toward the founding of educational systems and institutions. Parents not only made financial sacrifices; they also "voluntarily stripped themselves of the authority to educate their children in their own faith."[35] The children of Dissenters have become conformists, for the content of education has been "nonparental and nonreligious." The parents have been "starved of spiritual fellowship with their own children."[36] Living in a spiritual void, they have lost their authority:

> Is the void for the adult becoming intolerable? Is the helplessness of our attitude in this world crisis significant? Do our clubs, conventions, conferences lack inspiration? After all, authority comes from man's capacity of bowing to inspiration.[37]

Furthermore, if the adult does *not* communicate his moral and religious beliefs even in the home, and the content of education omits the most important matters, children will conclude that moral and religious beliefs are private, rather than social, concerns. When adults have lost their source of authority in a faith and wisdom to share, the accent is placed upon youth.

The church faces a dilemma concerning the role of the family in moral and religious education. It cannot accept parental responsibility without parental functions, and one of its tasks is to instruct parents in, and to train them for, their duties. On the other hand the authors of *Families in the Church* report that fewer than one in six of the parents interviewed wanted their children to remember most of all from their home life the Christian faith and the living of it, and only one in twenty wanted the children primarily to remember their moral training.[38] The investigators concluded that it is utopian at the present time to rely upon religious training in the family as the early church did in the secular world of that day:

> Church parents . . . do not regard themselves as direct teachers of their children in matters of Christian faith; they scarcely know what it is all about themselves. Without the church educating intensively at the adult level, as it did in the preparation of catechumens in the first centuries of its existence, there is little hope of home religious education being reinstated. Even with that kind of education, one wonders what can be accomplished in an urbanized culture in a family wherein the role of mother and father have changed drastically.[39]

Since the family and the church are both in crisis, it may be that what now seems impossible will become possible as moral and religious seriousness lead to the acceptance of varied responsibilities in moral and religious education.

A living tradition is not communicated from one generation to the next by simple and easy techniques. The process of acquiring a spiritual inheritance begins in the home, and is carried on in the church, the school, and other institutions which express our convictions and our aspirations. Impersonal methods of instruction are not enough. "It is from one man to another that the heavenly bread of self-being is passed," as Martin Buber has said.[40]

The church has a distinctive role in teaching the values that matter most. It is the only institution that has a lifelong opportunity to teach and to inspire. It binds us together as families and not merely as individuals. If it understands its task, it will not take over the functions of parents, or teachers, or government officials, or social workers. Rather it will seek to inspire them for their tasks, and ask of them responsibility to God as well as to man. The church offers a distinctive fellowship because it experiences a divine depth and height in life, and the power and enthusiasm of faith and limitless devotion. It provides the setting for the appearance of prophets and mystics and saints and courageous men and women who will die rather than lose freedom of worship and conscience. Although it is divided, it points beyond itself to our Creator and our common destiny. It seeks to direct our ways toward brotherhood and peace. It unites the generations with ties of faith and purpose. Its rightful claims are not for itself but for God. No other institution is ready to take the place of the church as the inspirer and transformer of human motives and conduct, for the sake of God and man.

NOTES

CHAPTER I. *Morals and Moral Education in America Today*

1. F. S. C. Northrop, *Meeting of East and West* (The Macmillan Company, 1946), p. 1.

2. Rev. Raymond C. Baumhart, S.J., in a survey published in the *Harvard Business Review* and summarized in *Time,* July 21, 1961, p. 66.

3. Henry Steele Commager, "We Have Changed—and Must," in *The New York Times Magazine,* April 30, 1961, pp. 10 ff.

4. Philip E. Jacob, *Changing Values in College* (Harper & Brothers, 1957), p. 2.

5. *Ibid.,* p. 2.

6. *Information Service,* Bureau of Research and Survey, National Council of the Churches of Christ in the U.S.A., Vol. XXXVII, No. 17 (October 25, 1958), p. 1.

7. Marjorie Carpenter, ed., *The Larger Learning* (W. C. Brown Company, 1960), Ch. 4, "Student Values," by John Bushnell, p. 56.

8. Dean Thomas S. Hall, in addressing the National Conference on Higher Education, reported in the St. Louis *Post-Dispatch* (March 9, 1960).

9. In *Religion and the Free Society,* a pamphlet published by The Fund for the Republic, Inc. (1958), p. 7.

10. Charles Morris, *Varieties of Human Value* (University of Chicago Press, 1956), pp. 43 ff.

11. Carpenter, *op. cit.,* p. 54.

12. Shepard B. Clough, *Basic Values of Western Civilization* (Columbia University Press, 1960), pp. 15 ff.

13. Bernard Mayo, *Ethics and the Moral Life* (Macmillan & Co., Ltd., London, 1958), p. 204.

14. Edward D. Eddy, Jr., and others, *College Influence on Student Character* (American Council on Education, 1959), p. 118.

15. Rose K. Goldsen, Morris Rosenberg, Robin M. Williams, Jr., and Edward A. Suchman, *What College Students Think* (D. Van Nostrand Company, Inc., 1960), pp. 75, 76.

16. Joseph M. Hopkins, "Cheating Is Symptomatic," in *The Presbyterian Outlook*, Feb. 20, 1961, p. 5.

17. "The College Student," prepared by Editorial Projects for Education, Inc., for printing in college and university alumni bulletins, printed in *The Miami Alumnus*, April, 1961.

18. Carpenter, *op. cit.*, p. 51.

19. Goldsen and others, *op. cit.*, p. 200.

20. Jacob, *op. cit.*, p. 2.

21. Morris, *op. cit.*, pp. 45 and 93.

22. Goldsen and others, *op. cit.*, p. 155.

23. *Ibid.*, p. 168.

24. Jacob, *op. cit.*, p. 4.

25. Morris, *op. cit.*, p. 69.

26. Clough, *op. cit.*, p. 8.

27. Henri Bergson, *The Two Sources of Morality and Religion* (Holt, Rinehart & Winston, Inc., 1935), p. 291.

28. George Santayana, *Character and Opinion in the United States* (George Braziller, Inc., 1955), p. 104.

29. Max Lerner, *America as a Civilization* (Simon and Schuster, Inc., 1957), p. 674.

30. *Prospect for America,* The Rockefeller Panel Reports (Doubleday & Co., Inc., 1961), p. 390.

31. Roy W. Fairchild and John Charles Wynn, *Families in the Church: A Protestant Survey* (Association Press, 1961), p. 18.

32. This quotation is taken from an article published by Dr. Mead about the year 1947, to which the reference has been lost.

33. Ralph Henry Gabriel, *Course of American Democratic Thought,* 2d ed. (The Ronald Press Company, 1956), p. 14.

34. *Ibid.*, p. 20.

35. *Ibid.*, p. 20.

36. *Ibid.*, p. 25.

37. *Ibid.*, p. 39.

38. *Ibid.*, p. 39.

39. Clough, *op. cit.*, p. 15.

40. *Ibid.*, pp. 43 and 45.

41. *Ibid.*, p. 24.

42. J. Robert Oppenheimer, *The Open Mind* (Simon and Schuster, Inc., 1955), p. 125.

43. Charles Morris, *Paths of Life* (George Braziller, Inc., 1956), p. 193.

44. Gerald Gurin, Joseph Veroff, and Sheila Feld, *Americans View Their Mental Health* (Basic Books, Inc., 1960), p. xv.

45. *Union Seminary Quarterly Review,* Vol. XV, No. 3 (March, 1960), p. 209.

46. General Assembly of The United Presbyterian Church in the U.S.A., Buffalo, New York, May 17–24, 1961, report of the Special Committee on National Purpose, *Minutes of the General Assembly,* Sixth Series, Volume IV, Part I, 1961.

47. Lerner, *op. cit.*, p. 657, and also p. 664.

CHAPTER II. *What Morality Is*

1. Amos 3:3, KJV.

2. Michael Polanyi, *Personal Knowledge* (University of Chicago Press, 1958), p. 215.

3. Aristotle, The Works of Aristotle Translated Into English, Vol. X, *Politica* (Oxford University Press, Inc., 1921), Book I, 2, p. 1253a.

4. Thomas Hobbes, *Leviathan,* Everyman's Library (J. M. Dent & Sons, 1937), p. 65.

5. *The Confessions of Saint Augustine,* Book I, XII, 19.

6. Deut. 5:17.

7. Bergson, *op. cit.*, p. 12.

8. Ralph Barton Perry, *Realms of Value* (Harvard University Press, 1954), p. 164.

9. Albert Camus, in *Mademoiselle,* May, 1960.

10. Kurt Baier, *The Moral Point of View* (Cornell University Press, 1958), p. 215.

11. *Ibid.*, p. 170.

12. William Ernest Hocking, *The Self: Its Body and Freedom*

(Yale University Press, 1928), p. 67.

13. Reported in the St. Louis *Post-Dispatch,* June 28, 1961.

14. Clarence Irving Lewis, *An Analysis of Knowledge and Valuation* (The Open Court Publishing Company, 1947), p. 481.

15. Baier, *op. cit.,* p. 106.

16. Matt. 7:12.

17. Immanuel Kant, *Metaphysics of Morals,* First Section, p. 48.

18. Quoted by Philip Wheelwright in *A Critical Introduction to Ethics,* 3d ed. (Odyssey Press, 1959), p. 222.

19. Langdon B. Gilkey, "Excerpts from an Internment Camp Journal," *Christianity and Crisis,* Vol. VI, No. 9 (May 27, 1946), p. 6.

20. *Ibid.*

21. Hobbes, *op. cit.,* p. 64.

22. Plato, *The Apology,* 28.

23. *Ibid.,* 30.

24. Matt. 6:33.

25. Bergson, *op. cit.,* p. 12.

26. A. E. Taylor, *The Faith of a Moralist* (Macmillan & Co., Ltd., London, 1931), Series I, p. 389, in the one-volume edition, 1937.

CHAPTER III. *Moral Education*

1. Baier, *op. cit.,* p. 257.

2. Perry, *op. cit.,* p. 429.

3. *Ibid.,* p. 429.

4. *Ibid.,* p. 430.

5. *Politica,* Book VII, 15, p. 1334b.

6. Aristotle, The Works of Aristotle Translated Into English, Vol. IX, *Ethica Nichomachea* (Oxford University Press, Inc., 1925), Book II, 1, p. 1103 a,b.

7. *Ibid.,* p. 1103b.

8. *An Autobiography,* p. 15, quoted in T. V. Smith's *Constructive Ethics* (Appleton-Century-Crofts, Inc., 1948), p. 37.

9. J. B. Pratt, *The Religious Consciousness* (The Macmillan Company, 1927), p. 108.

10. An experimental curriculum has been developed for use in some churches that may be considered an exception to this statement. See Ernest M. Ligon, *Dimensions of Character* (The Mac-

millan Company, 1956), for a description of the Union College Character Research Project.

11. Gordon W. Allport, *Becoming* (Yale University Press, 1935), pp. 70, 71.

12. Julian Huxley, *New Bottles for New Wine* (Harper & Brothers, 1957), p. 231.

13. F. E. Sparshott, *An Enquiry Into Goodness* (University of Chicago Press, 1958), p. 294.

14. Sören Kierkegaard, *Either/Or*, Vol. II, tr. by Walter Lowrie (Doubleday & Company, Inc., 1959), p. 188.

15. *Ibid.*, p. 220.

16. William Ernest Hocking, *The Coming World Civilization* (Harper & Brothers, 1956), p. 7.

17. Eddy, *op. cit.*, p. 9.

18. Herbert W. Schneider, *Morals for Mankind* (University of Missouri Press, 1960), p. 14.

19. George Bernard Shaw, *The Intelligent Woman's Guide to Socialism and Capitalism* (Brentano's, Inc., 1928), p. 364.

20. Donald Walhout, "Why Should I Be Moral?—A Reconsideration," *The Review of Metaphysics*, Vol. XII, No. 4, Issue No. 48 (June, 1959), p. 585.

21. I Cor. 12:31.

22. Philip E. Mosely, "How the Kremlin Keeps Ivan in Line," *The New York Times Magazine*, February 19, 1961.

23. See Chapter I, p. 38.

24. Perry, *op. cit.*, p. 156.

25. Union College Studies in Character Research, *Historical Introduction* (published by The Character Research Project), p. 22.

26. Harry S. Broudy, *Building a Philosophy of Education* (Prentice-Hall, Inc., 1954), p. 407.

27. St. Louis *Post-Dispatch*, June 26, 1960.

28. Crane Brinton, *A History of Western Morals* (Harcourt, Brace & World, Inc., 1959), p. 417.

29. See note 10 in this chapter.

30. Lerner, *op. cit.*, p. 530.

CHAPTER IV. *"Moralism" and Moral Education*

1. *Webster's New Collegiate Dictionary* (G. & C. Merriam Co., 1956).

2. Fritz-Joachim von Rintelen, "Existence–Self-transcendence," in *Self, Religion, and Metaphysics*, ed. by Gerald E. Myers (The Macmillan Company, 1961), p. 48.

3. C. G. Jung, *The Undiscovered Self* (Little, Brown & Company, 1958), pp. 53 f.

4. Francis J. Rigney and L. Douglas Smith, *The Real Bohemia* (Basic Books, Inc., 1961), pp. xv and xvii.

5. Sören Kierkegaard, *Training in Christianity*, tr. by Walter Lowrie (Princeton University Press, 1944), p. 87.

6. Rollo May, in *Existence*, ed. by Rollo May, Ernest Angel, and Henri F. Ellenberger (Basic Books, Inc., 1958), p. 45. Italics in the original.

7. Alphonse Maeder, *Ways to Psychic Health* (Charles Scribner's Sons, 1953), p. 27.

8. Paul Tillich, *Theology of Culture* (Oxford University Press, Inc., 1959), pp. 114–124.

9. John Dillenberger, in *The Christian Century*, June 3, 1959, p. 668.

10. Reinhold Niebuhr, in *Christianity and Crisis*, Vol. XXI, No. 11 (June 26, 1961), p. 109.

11. Reinhold Niebuhr, in *The Christian Century*, July 15, 1936, p. 985.

12. *Ibid.*, p. 986.

13. Mark 12:31.

14. Reinhold Niebuhr, in *The Christian Century*, July 15, 1936, p. 987.

15. H. Richard Niebuhr, *The Meaning of Revelation* (The Macmillan Company, 1941), p. 29.

16. Reported in *Time*, July 14, 1961.

17. Tillich, *op. cit.*, p. 138.

18. Morton White, *Religion, Politics, and the Higher Learning* (Harvard University Press, 1959), p. 6.

19. Robert Ulich, *Philosophy of Education* (American Book Company, 1961), p. 133.

20. O. Herbert Mowrer, in *The American Psychologist*, Vol. XV, No. 5 (May, 1960), p. 303.

21. See Chapter I, p. 15.

22. Emil Brunner, *The Divine Imperative*, tr. by Olive Wyon (The Westminster Press, 1947), p. 115.

23. Matt. 5:48.

24. John Knox, *The Ethic of Jesus in the Teaching of the Church* (Abingdon Press, 1961), pp. 22, 23.

25. Ulich, *op. cit.*, p. 20.

26. Augustine, *Enchiridion,* Ch. cxvii, quoted in *Christian Ethics,* H. Richard Niebuhr and Waldo Beach, eds. (The Ronald Press Company, 1955), p. 108.

27. Matt. 7:16.

CHAPTER V. *Religion, the Church, and Moral Education*

1. See Crane Brinton, *A History of Western Morals,* p. 28.

2. Richard von Mises, *Positivism* (George Braziller, Inc., 1956), p. 370.

3. *Ibid.,* p. 351.

4. George H. Sabine, *A History of Political Theory,* 1st ed. (Holt, Rinehart & Winston, Inc., 1937), p. 180.

5. *Ibid.,* p. 185.

6. Niccolo Machiavelli, *The Prince,* tr. by Luigi Ricci (Oxford University Press, London, 1935), p. 65.

7. John Bennett, *Christianity and Our World,* Hazen Books on Religion (Association Press, 1936), p. 33.

8. St. Louis *Post-Dispatch,* April 19, 1959.

9. C. Wright Mills, *The Power Elite* (Oxford University Press, Inc., 1956), p. 6.

10. Will Herberg, *Protestant—Catholic—Jew* (Doubleday & Co., Inc., 1955), pp. 51–53.

11. "Religious Revival and Moral Crisis," *Union Seminary Quarterly Review,* Vol. XV, No. 3 (March, 1960), p. 211.

12. Sydney E. Ahlstrom, "Theology in America: A Historical Survey," p. 319 in *The Shaping of American Religion,* Vol. I in Religion in American Life, ed. by James Ward Smith and A. Leland Jamison (Princeton University Press, 1961).

13. Fairchild, *op. cit.,* p. 169.

14. *Ibid.,* p. 175.

15. Goldsen, *op. cit.,* p. 176.

16. Hans Hofmann, ed., *Making the Ministry Relevant* (Charles Scribner's Sons, 1960), Ch. 2, "The Relevance of the Ministry in Our Time and Its Theological Foundation," by Paul Tillich, p. 23.

17. Abraham H. Maslow, ed., *New Knowledge in Human Values,* Part I, "The Powers of Creative Unselfish Love," by Pitirim A. Sorokin, p. 4.

18. Taylor, *op. cit.,* p. 12.

19. Kierkegaard, *Training in Christianity,* p. 67.

20. Johannes Hamel, in *How to Serve God in a Marxist Land* (Association Press, 1959), p. 117.

21. Joseph Sittler, *The Structure of Christian Ethics* (Louisiana State University Press, 1958), p. 19.

22. Georg Brochmann, *Humanity and Happiness,* tr. by Frank G. Nelson (The Viking Press, Inc., 1950), p. 163.

23. H. Richard Niebuhr, *The Meaning of Revelation* (The Macmillan Company, 1946), p. viii.

24. Gabriel Marcel, *Man Against Mass Society,* tr. by G. S. Fraser (Henry Regnery Company, 1952), p. 3.

25. See Chapter I, note 24.

26. Mark 8:35.

27. Dietrich Bonhoeffer, *Ethics,* tr. by Neville Horton Smith (The Macmillan Company, 1955), p. 5.

28. Acts 5:29.

29. Goldsen, *op. cit.,* p. 165.

30. Matt. 5:8.

31. I John 4:20.

32. John 7:16–17.

33. See note 18 in this chapter.

34. John Baillie, *Our Knowledge of God* (Charles Scribner's Sons, 1939), p. 4.

35. Thatcher Winslow and Frank P. Davidson, eds., *American Youth* (Harvard University Press, 1940), Ch. 1, "Youth and Authority," by Eugen Rosenstock-Huessy, pp. 4–8.

36. *Ibid.,* pp. 9, 10.

37. *Ibid.,* p. 12.

38. Fairchild, *op. cit.,* p. 138.

39. *Ibid.,* p. 105.

40. Martin Buber, *To Hallow This Life,* an anthology, ed. by Jacob Trapp (Harper & Brothers, 1958), p. 25.

INDEX